Pillars

Aaron O'Harra

Table of Contents

Acknowledgements

I write for you, *Redeemer Fellowship*. Your faces are the backdrop to every word written in this book. One of my hopes in *Pillars* is that you would feel our love and care for you by unrelentingly pointing you to the glory of our eternal God in the face of the risen Christ. We elders labor together for your complete joy in him. (Philippians 2:2) I'm thankful that two of your brothers, Jordan Scarbrough and Dave Baker, have joined in this effort by writing both the Foreword and Afterword.

Regarding this project, I first want to begin by thanking my wife, Jena. You've truly been an anchor in all seasons of my ministry, and not just in the books that I have written. The labors of a pastor are often misunderstood because they're not quantifiable, nor are the struggles that come along with it. And you bear it all with me. So, thank you Jena, for exemplifying these pillars of God's truth in your ministry to me and our children. You are precious in the sight of God. (1 Peter 3:4)

I also want to thank the elders of *Redeemer Fellowship*, for not only bearing the load in my four-week absence to create the majority of the content of this book, but for being a constant source of strength and support for all of us, in your prayer and teaching. I would want every person reading this to know that these men do far more than most think, or will ever hear about. They are men whom I admire, as they labor in secret for their reward from their heavenly Father. (Matthew 6:4-6)

Thank you also Connie Baker, who spent hours going through each chapter, correcting my many mistakes and working meticulously to create the Scripture Index. Your attention to detail is incredible and I was continually impressed with both your insights and willingness to take on both of these monumental tasks.

Thank you Chad and Haylie Reeves, who worked on the cover and summary text in addition to graphics and illustrations for both *Pillars* and *Redeemer Fellowship's Affirmation of Faith*. Your work gives an excellent aesthetic that complements the contents of both works. You both have a gift and I pray that the Lord blesses you in it in the years to come.

To you, *Redeemer Fellowship*, you are a blessed church body and unique in the sight of God. I pray that you would stand on the pillars of God's truth in Christ for the building up of his body, both in our generation, and the generations to come.

Pastor Aaron

To Redeemer Fellowship
The Beloved of God

Foreword

You hold in your hands an instrument of worship. *Pillars* was born out of what is now *Redeemer Fellowship's Affirmation of Faith*, which is a collection of historic Christian doctrines that form the foundation of our local church. When the elders of the former church, *The Rising*, began composing our *Affirmation of Faith*, they invited me to contribute as an elder apprentice. Three years later, having transitioned into the office of elder, I was delighted to see this *Bible*-saturated work come to fruition for the benefit of God's people, both now and in the generations to come. My hope is that it will be a robust instrument for personal, family, and congregational worship, to the glory of God among the nations.

The Christian life is worship. Beginning on a personal level, my aim with *Pillars* is that these essential truths would be a vehicle that drives us in worship of Jesus and conformity to his image, daily growing in his grace and our knowledge of him. With the help of the Holy Spirit, I expect that the theology in this book will move our hearts and minds to doxology—to a greater affection for God.

But my hope for *Pillars* lies not only here. This book is also intended to extend from personal worship into family worship—an essential practice in Christian discipleship. Just as the Hebrews were instructed in Deuteronomy 6:7 to talk of God's word while walking, sitting down, lying down, and rising, my hope is that the families of *Redeemer Fellowship* would follow in their footsteps. In your reading, ask questions together. Memorize the Scriptures cited together. Pray together as a family—that the Lord would lead you into deeper love for him and for one another.

And just as personal and family worship define the Christian life, congregational worship defines the Church's life. Oh that *Pillars* would become a powerful tool in making disciples in the local church, and strengthen the bride of Christ for the work of the ministry. Every member of our church has the responsibility to pursue individual maturity, so as to contribute to the collective maturity of the whole. *Pillars,* under the authority of Scripture, acts as a guide for clearly defining who belongs in this congregation. In turn, this works toward our collective worship as we encourage and hold one another accountable—with each person contributing, the elders overseeing, and Christ ruling as head.

But what value is this instrument of worship if it's only heard within the walls of our local church? These truths are intended to resound to the ends of the earth. The Great Composer is orchestrating his Kingdom to span across every tongue, tribe, nation and people. With the help of the Holy Spirit, my heart is zealous that *Pillars* would propel us to fulfill the Great Commission given by our Lord Jesus as we bring his good news to the world.

With love for Christ and his Church,

Jordan Baxter Scarbrough

Preface

This is a companion book. *Pillars* originally was a sermon series where I explained every point of *The Affirmation of Faith*, which the elders had composed over the course of four years. After the initial full draft of that document, we felt it necessary to give a sermon series that explained each affirmation. The result of that sermon series, after refining the meat of what was taught during those Sundays, is what you now hold in your hands—*Pillars*. So, in a sense, this is two works contained in one. This book is both *The Affirmation of Faith* and the explanation of that affirmation.

One important aspect to *Pillars*, is that I have included the affirmation within the book by placing each statement at the beginning of each chapter. This gives you, the reader, an opportunity to read the statement first, and have all the *Scripture* references available before you begin reading the contents of that chapter. Be ready to examine each *Scripture* reference and each statement with attentiveness.

Another important aspect of these two works is that each statement builds upon the previous one and therefore each chapter does as well. There are two implications of this that are worth noting.

The first is that we aren't communicating value in the order of each statement. Just because one statement precedes the other, it doesn't follow that it's more important. For example, we begin the entire book with *The Bible* because it is through God's Word that we know God—which is why we then move toward our second statement on the nature of God. This, however, does not mean that we value *The Bible* more than God. But it does mean that in order to know God, we need to hear him speak first.

The second implication of the ordering is that it shouldn't be treated as a systematic theology book, flipping back and forth between chapters. The chapters are not intended to stand-alone. For the best understanding of the contents of this book, my hope is that you begin with the first pillar and end with the last.

Lastly, and probably most important, is to remember that before you open these pages and explore the central teachings of the Christian faith, ask the Lord Jesus to lead you in worshipping him. My aim is that in this theologically oriented book, you would find joy in our glorious God as you open his Word and gaze at his beauty. Theology to doxology.

Introduction
Why Pillars?

Redeemer Fellowship's Affirmation of Faith

Theology matters. What we believe sets the course of our lives. Knowing this, in 2014 the elders began the task of formulating the central doctrines of our church in what is now known as *The Affirmation of Faith*. What is an affirmation of faith? It's a document written by the elders of our church that places contours on the core doctrines that shape and mold our identity—doctrines that we believe are central to the gospel message of our Lord Jesus Christ and therefore vital to the Christian Church.

So why do we need an affirmation of faith? Our elders recognize that *The Bible* makes distinctions between those who *are not* Christians and those who are. And the way *The Bible* distinguishes between the Christian and non-Christian is not only in the conduct of one's life, but also, and more fundamentally, the truths they adhere to. The purpose of this *Affirmation of Faith* is to identify those truths that constitute a genuine Christian—a true disciple of Jesus.

Although the words "Affirmation of Faith" are never mentioned in *The Bible*, at the same time it develops these same doctrinal distinctions. For example, the Apostle Paul says in Galatians 1:6,

> 6 I am astonished that you are so quickly deserting him who called you in the grace of Christ and are turning to a *different gospel*—(Galatians 1:6; Emphasis Mine)[1]

With Paul, he understands that there are at least two types of "gospels" out there. There is true information and there is false information, and it appears that the Galatians embraced the wrong one. If we take a step back, in the very least we observe that Paul considers information and understanding to be of utmost importance. He continues in verses 7-9.

> 7 not that there is another one, but there are some who trouble you and want to *distort the gospel* of Christ. 8 But even if we or an angel from heaven should preach to you a gospel *contrary* to the one we preached to you, let him be accursed. 9 As we have said before, so now I say again: If anyone is preaching to you a gospel *contrary* to the one you received, let him be accursed. (Galatians 1:7-9)

Doctrine Matters

Paul's urgency shows us that doctrine matters. It really matters. Paul knows that what the Galatians think and *affirm* about God not only has earthly implications, but more-so, heavenly ones. Their understanding of God—their theology—mattered enough for him to curse those promoting a false gospel. He commands twice, "Let him be damned!" (Galatians 1:8-9)

But Paul's urgency doesn't end in chapter 1. We also see throughout the letter that some among the Galatians were teaching that the true disciples of Christ had to obey the law in order to be saved. Paul writes in chapter 5:

11 But if I, brothers, still preach circumcision, why am I still being persecuted? In that case the offense of the cross has been removed. 12 I wish those who unsettle you would emasculate themselves! (Galatians 5:11-12)

What Paul is essentially saying is: "If circumcision gets you right with God, than there's no need for the cross of Christ. If you really believe that cutting your foreskin off makes you righteous before God, then why stop at the foreskin? Go all the way and so prove your 'ultra-righteousness.'"

This is shocking language—obviously reserved for the most severe of cases. It's shocking because the distortion of the gospel message deserves such severity.

And so, what we witness in the Apostle Paul is earnestness for this church to stay within the theological boundaries of Christianity. In other words, he draws a doctrinal distinction that *affirms* the truth of the Christian faith—"This is what being a Christian is, and this is what it is not."

Do All Doctrines Matter?

Naturally, the follow-up question is: Do all doctrines *equally* matter? The short answer is *no*. Turn back a few pages from Galatians and we'll see that Paul didn't consider all doctrines equal. Just look at the Corinthians.

The Corinthians weren't distorting the gospel message like the Galatians were, but they had other problems. They had a hard time living out the doctrines they affirmed with their mouth. They were the rough-around-the-edges, riff-raff that would make a lot of present-day "Christians" uneasy. They were babies learning how to walk, and stumbling most of the way on the straight and narrow.

For example, the make-up of the Corinthian church consisted of a man having sex with his Dad's wife (1 Corinthians 5:1), church members suing one another (1 Corinthians 6:5-6), rivalries forming with different church leaders (1 Corinthians 1:12), and congregants getting drunk with the communion wine (1 Corinthians 11:21). Needless to say, these Corinthians weren't easy on the spiritual eyes. Yet Paul addresses them quite differently than he does the Galatians. He corrects them as he would a small child—with gentleness.

> 14 I do not write these things to make you ashamed, but to admonish you as my beloved children. 15 For though you have countless guides in Christ, you do not have many fathers. For I became your father in Christ Jesus through the gospel. 16 I urge you, then, be imitators of me. (1 Corinthians 4:14-16)

We should notice the patience in Paul's pastoral care. The sound of his voice is silk while his substance is stone. And lest we think this is an aberration, he again addresses them in the same manner in chapter 6.

11 And such were some of you. But you were washed, you were sanctified, you were justified in the name of the Lord Jesus Christ and by the Spirit of our God. (1 Corinthians 6:11)

Open-Handed vs. Close-Handed

So, why would Paul address these two churches differently? Why is there a sharp contrast between those in Galatia and those in Corinth?

With Paul, there are things worth enduring through, and then there are things worth dying for. With some doctrines, Paul would suffer through, patiently persistent in correction. But others, he would not. These two categories are often referred to as *"Open-Handed Doctrines"* and *"Close-Handed Doctrines."*

The Open-Handed Doctrines are beliefs that any one of us can put on the table with our burger, fries, and Pepsi and lovingly disagree on without breaking unity and fellowship—doctrines like, infant/believers baptism; speaking in tongues or not; pre-millennialism/post-millennialism/amillennialism; Calvinism and Arminianism; various Bible translations; young-earth creationism or old-earth creationism.

These are examples of theological hills that we may, or do in fact, disagree on and yet they are not hills that we would die on, or divide over.

So then what are the Close-Handed Doctrines? They are the *Affirmation of Faith* and the next ten chapters. They are the doctrinal hills that we are willing to die for. They are the doctrines that many in our Christian heritage have, in fact, died for. They are that important.

Unity

The upshot of all of this, both the *Affirmation of Faith* and *Pillars*, is that when we fully embrace the close-handed doctrines that are essential to the Christian life, and embrace them together, a unique bond is formed between us. The word for this is "unity".

> 11 And he gave the apostles, the prophets, the evangelists, the shepherds and teachers, 12 to equip the saints for the work of ministry, for building up the body of Christ, 13 until we all attain to *the unity of the faith and of the knowledge of the Son of God*, to mature manhood, to the measure of the stature of the fullness of Christ… (Ephesians 4:11-13)

Paul commands us to strive for unity in not only the faith, but also the *knowledge* of the Son of God so that we grow into the fullness of Jesus Christ himself. Unity sounds great. In fact, many people from many different religions could even champion this same unity in the knowledge of Jesus. But when it comes down to it, unity "of the knowledge of the Son of God" between different religions, is impossible.

Just imagine that certain leaders from Jehovah's Witnesses, Mormonism, Rastafarianism, Judaism, and a few Pentecostal snake-handlers all gathered around a large table and said, "Let's bring all our followers together and unite them in the knowledge of Jesus." And everyone would bang on the table in enthusiastic agreement. That sounds good, right?

But then, one of the leaders pulls out his pen and notepad and says, "Alright. Let's just jot down a few notes about who Jesus is, to get started. I mean, if we're going to unite in the knowledge of Jesus, we best agree on just the basics of whom he is, right?"

And so the Jehovah's Witness says, "I'll start. Let's begin with his real name—Michael, the Archangel."

And the Mormon looks at him and says, "Are you crazy? His name is Jesus. He's got a brother named Lucifer."

And the Rastafarian says, "Guys, he goes by the name of Haile Selassie, and he was the emperor of Ethiopia in the early 1900's."

And the Jew says, "He's none of those. His real name is Joshua, and wasn't an angel. He wasn't a spiritual brother of Lucifer. He doesn't live today in Ethiopia. He was a great prophet, and nothing more."

And then the other guy doesn't know what any of them are talking about and so he just throws a bunch of snakes on the table. This sure doesn't sound like unity does it?

In this example, all of these religions took their version of Jesus and sought unity, but couldn't even agree on the basics of Jesus. What this demonstrates is the necessity for an *Affirmation of Faith* when pursuing unity with one another in the knowledge of the Son of God. We must agree on who Jesus is. Which "Jesus" are we striving to unite under?

There are many people who say, "I believe in Jesus." And an affirmation of faith answers the question, "Which one?" The Jesus of Mormonism is very different than that of Christianity, despite having a similar appearance. In fact, this is how deception works.

It's like biting into a Bavarian cream donut, thinking it was lemon all along. On the outside, they both look the same, but the more we approach the middle, the more we realize how different they are. We are still talking about donuts right?

The same is true with regard to who we believe Jesus was and is. If the central components of the middle are different, we can expect our worship and enjoyment of God to be different as well. The *Affirmation of Faith* and this complementary book, *Pillars*, labor to bring clarity to the center of the proverbial donut, and so be unified in the knowledge of the true Son of God. (Ephesians 4:13)

Identification

How this *Affirmation of Faith* serves our church is that we are now able to draw lines between those who worship God truly in Christ, and those who don't. We are able to look out on fellow congregants and identify those who belong to the body of Christ, and those who don't. Now, why in the world would we want to do that? It sounds kind of mean.

First, it's not so that we can identify the non-Christians and shoo them away, so as to prevent infecting everyone else who comes to church on Sunday. That's not it. Rather, this would have the opposite effect. We would want to pursue them in a different way than those within the boundaries of the church. We would pray fervently for God "to open their eyes, so that they may turn from darkness to light." (Acts 26:18) Such a document helps us in our prayers and interactions with those outside the boundaries of the Christian faith.

But while we desire for non-Christians to come through our doors—to meet them, take them to lunch, pray for them, love them—we also desire to differentiate between *family*, *friend*, and possibly *foe*.

> 18 For through him we both have access in one Spirit to the Father. 19 So then you are no longer strangers and aliens, but you are fellow citizens with the saints and members of the household of God... (Ephesians 2:18-19)

> 10 So then, as we have opportunity, let us do good to everyone, and especially to those who are of the household of faith. (Galatians 6:10)

Passages like these demonstrate how we interact with the two groups of people, and the *Affirmation of Faith* clarifies who belongs to what group—who is family and who is friend—whom we are to be "especially" good to—whom we are to hold accountable—whom we are to celebrate the Lord's Table with.

Wisdom in Clarity

The *Affirmation of Faith* also functions as a vehicle for transparency. Sometimes we can use vague language either to entrap others or conceal our true meaning. This is demonstrated almost daily on any major news network. You know the scene: two radicals are pitted against each other and all we hear are misleading words, logical fallacies, and savvy-ness with language.

This is not what we, as Christians, are called to be. We are called to honest speech and clarity, because we know that we will give an account for every careless word spoken. (Matthew 12:36)

Former elder, Dave Baker, has said before, "If I ask someone in the church, 'What do you believe?' and he says, 'I believe the whole-counsel of God.' That would probably create more questions than answers." Such a response is inadequate and actually gives the appearance that this individual is hiding something. The vagueness in his answer creates more uncertainty.

We don't want to be this way. We are called to be "above reproach." (1 Timothy 3:2) Therefore, to fend off the appearance of any secrecy, we run from ambiguity. We labor to "not shrink from declaring to you the whole counsel of God..." (Acts 20:27) while at the same time desiring to "take pains to have a clear conscience toward both God and man." (Acts 24:16) So we lay this *Affirmation of Faith*, and *Pillars*, in the light before *Redeemer Fellowship* in our best terms possible for all to witness and judge.

Pillars

Now, the question becomes, "What are these central doctrines?" What are the beliefs worth dying for? What are these truths that are so important that if taken away, they destroy the vitality of the Church?

We have identified them as doctrinal pillars. They are the supports of the Christian faith—the foundational beliefs that are explicated in *The Bible* and affirmed throughout Christian history.

Jesus says in Matthew 16:18, "I will build my church!" And the foundation that Jesus lays is the very confession and belief that Peter utters. "You are the Christ, the Son of the living God." (Matthew 16:16)

The entire Church of Christ Jesus is built upon this confession —this affirmation. And if the building is supported by this foundation, then we must be careful to identify each pillar contained in it. We must know, who is the Christ?

So what are these Pillars that make up the foundation of Jesus Christ and his Church? We have ten of them—a chapter devoted to each:

Pillar 1: The Bible

Pillar 2: God

Pillar 3: God the Father

Pillar 4: God the Son

Pillar 5: God the Holy Spirit

Pillar 6: Humanity and Its Destiny

Pillar 7: Humanity and Salvation

Pillar 8: Satan

Pillar 9: The Church

Pillar 10: The Return of Jesus

So let's get busy. Let's kneel down in the dirt and examine the craftsmanship of this foundation, beholding the pillars and marveling at the beauty and wisdom of the Great Builder.

Introduction Endnotes

[1] All scriptures are taken from *The Holy Bible: English Standard Version* (Wheaton, IL: Crossway, 2001)

Pillar 1
The Bible

Affirmation

We believe that the sixty-six books of the Old and New Testaments are God's Word[1], written through men[2], by inspiration of the Holy Spirit[3]. Therefore, *The Bible* is infallible—as originally given,[4] essential for instruction in faith and practice,[5] and the sufficient revelation of Christ Jesus. Therefore, the Word of God is our final authority[6].

[1] Corinthians 14:37; Psalm 119; [2] 1 Peter 2:21; [3] 2 Timothy 3:16;
[4] Psalm 12:6; [5] Romans 15:4; 2 Timothy 3:14-16; Luke 24:27, 44-45;
Acts 17:2-3; 2 Peter 3:16; [6] Hebrews 4:12

What is The Bible?

We begin our *Affirmation of Faith* with *The Bible*.[1] What is it? What's its make-up? What's so special about this book? Why is *The Bible* the first of our pillars?

Let's begin with the basic question: What is *The Bible*? Historically, *The Bible* is a book that is a collection of 66 books that have been divided into two major volumes, commonly referred to as *The Old Testament* and *The New Testament*. Within these 66 books are a number of different authors and genres, having been written on three major continents, in three different languages, covering thousands of years. So, why do we have these 66 books, and not others? Who decided that these would be included in *The Bible*?

The 66 Books

Regarding *The Old Testament*, Jesus himself believed that the 39 books were God's inspired word—nothing more and nothing less. So if we're asked, "Why are these Old Testament books considered to be God's Word?" The short answer is that Jesus believed they were God's Word, and if Jesus believed it, we do as well.

Regarding the other 27 books of *The New Testament*, we believe they are God's Inspired Word because they were written by those who personally knew Jesus, or written by those who recorded their accounts, as in the case of Luke. These writings were not only completed within the first century of Jesus' life, death and resurrection, but they were also confirmed by the Apostles,[2] eyewitnesses, and the collective Church for hundreds of years after.

This ongoing process of confirming the validity of these documents and their truthfulness is known as *canonization*. Canonization is the standard that the historic Christian Church has used to determine what qualifies and disqualifies certain writings as God's inspired word. From the initial birth of *The New Testament* until the fourth century, the Christian Church had put these writings through this process, and what resulted were these 27 books of *The New Testament* that we now possess—nothing more and nothing less.

Written Through Men

Our *Affirmation of Faith* continues by explaining how we got these writings. We say, "written through men". By saying this, we are both recognizing that humans were the authors, while also attributing ultimate authorship to the *Great Author*—God himself. The way these words have come onto the pages of *The Bible* is through the *agency* of mankind. Peter affirms this very thing in his second letter.

> 21 For no prophecy was ever produced by the will of man, but men spoke from God as they were carried along by the Holy Spirit. (2 Peter 1:21)

Every word contained in *The Bible* has come through the means of human beings. These words didn't fall from heaven onto a page written in some celestial script. They came through humans with human language. God has chosen to use his creatures to communicate to his creatures about himself.

The infinite God could have written a book, plopped it down right in front of us and told us to read it. But that's not the way he works. While God is the author of this book, the means by which he writes comes through the hands of his image-bearers. God has, in a sense, partnered with humanity in revealing himself to humanity.

This is amazing, isn't it? The infinite God profoundly involves himself with his finite creatures. The fact that *The Bible* is written by God, through men, displays both his transcendence and immanence—his infinite being working through finite beings—his power displayed through vessels of weakness. (2 Corinthians 12:9)

So when asked, "Did God write *The Bible* or did men?" We can confidently answer with a resounding, "Yes!" God wrote this book through men.

By Inspiration of the Holy Spirit

Now "through" becomes a very important word at this point and it should be distinguished with the word "by". As we move to the next phrase we'll understand this a bit more. Our affirmation continues: "by inspiration of the Holy Spirit."

As to the question earlier: What's so special about this book? This is what makes *The Bible* so special. While *The Bible* came *through* men, it didn't come *by* men. *The Bible* came by God. *The Bible* says about itself that it's *inspired*. This means that God's Holy Spirit spoke to men in ways that compelled them to write down what he was speaking to them. Paul uses this word *"inspiration"* in his second letter to Timothy.

All Scripture is *breathed out* by God and profitable for teaching, for reproof, for correction, and for training in righteousness… (2 Timothy 3:16)

The term Paul uses in 2 Timothy is "breathed out". Some translations use the word "inspired". Either way, both communicate that the *Scriptures* come from the inner being of God. By God's breath came the very *Word of God—The Bible* we have today. God is the source of the truths written on these thin pages, bound in leather.

Infallible

And since *The Bible* is from God, breathed out by him, and God himself is perfect, then it follows that his word is also perfect. The entirety of God's Word is flawless.

> 7 The Law of the LORD is perfect,
> reviving the soul;
> the testimony of the LORD is sure,
> making wise the simple.
> (Psalms 19:7)

This is why our statement affirms that "*The Bible* is infallible…" We believe it is without error. The *Word of God* is perfect in every way and cannot be false or contradictory.

Is The Bible Contradictory?

Now, the skeptics may laugh at a statement like this, because it's apparent to them that *The Bible* is full of contradictions. But more often than not, such a statement is offered with dishonesty and carelessness with the text. This dishonesty and carelessness is not only a problem in religious circles, but in every day life as well.

We human beings naturally assume we have an accurate understanding of someone else's ideas and rarely see ourselves as having an interpretive problem. What it comes down to is this: If we don't understand something…"It's always their fault."

But the wise listener is also the prudent one. The wise are slow to trust their own understanding. This especially applies to reading the *Scriptures*. The wise, when opening *The Bible* and coming across two passages of Scripture that seem contradictory, would assume fallibility in themselves. Despite the mantra of today: "Trust your heart," the wise one knows that his heart often leads him astray, as does his mind. The wise one knows that *we* are the problem, and not *The Bible*. So what ground do I have to say this as it regards to contradictions in *Scripture*?

One of the common arguments for the unreliability of *The Bible* is that there are so many different religions, denominations, and even translations of *The Bible*. It's a book so unclear that nobody can agree on it. The argument goes something like this:

> "*The Bible* can't be understood. Look at all the different interpretations, let alone all the sects, cults, and denominations that stem from it. If this book were so perfect, then why can't anybody agree on it? It sure doesn't seem reliable to me."

I would suggest that this scenario does in fact speak to unreliability—but not of the book. It says a whole lot about the unreliability of people.

Doug Wilson, in a debate with Dan Barker, once illustrated this.[3] He argued that if we take the *same* Bible and hand it to five individuals and put them in five separate rooms, after having read it, they would walk out with twelve denominations.

In this scenario we should be looking for the variable in the experiment. Wilson argues that the different interpretations that came from the *same* text make a case for the unreliability of people and not the unreliability of the text. The only variable between them was that the people were different. As the old adage says, "To error is human."

The Blessing of Humility

Now, assuming our own inadequacies is not a bad thing. Sure, our ego takes a hit, especially if we pride ourselves in our intellect. But assuming our own weakness in understanding a divinely inspired text actually sets us up for a healthy labor in the text—a mental tilling of the soil of *Scripture* that will yield an abundance of fruit within our souls. In other words, hard texts push us to think hard. And thinking on the infallible, pure, and perfect Word of God always produces abundant fruit.

Originally Given

But you'll notice in our affirmation there is a *caveat* to all this. Our statement continues, "…as originally given." Why this phrase?

The fact is, there are no original manuscripts of *The Bible* that exist today. What we have, in terms of historical documents, are copies of copies—and a lot of copies at that. And as is with the transmission of any text, with copies also come errors. So how can we say that *The Bible* is infallible if in the texts we now have there are so many errors? The short answer is that while the copies have errors, the originals didn't. I know what you're saying, "How is that?"

We have to remember that at the time of *The Bible* there was no such thing as a copy machines, a Word Document, or email. Even the primitive form of that technology didn't exist until the printing press in the 15th century. So, for over a thousand years, people copied by hand. And we can imagine the propensity to error when writing by hand. We find it difficult to write an email without errors when it has spell and grammar check already built in.

Their methods of copying varied as well. For example, when scribes would copy *The Bible* they could copy directly from one-page to the next. Other times a reader would stand in a room full of scribes and read the text while everyone wrote down what they heard. Sometimes scribes would have the text memorized and write it all down from memory. (Good luck with that!) So we can imagine the human error involved in tasks involved with copying by hand.

But it was through these methods of copying, and other methods as well, that *The Bible* was transmitted, with the result being the thousands of manuscripts or fragments of scripture we now possess today.[4] And most of these contain discrepancies—most of which are small and not big enough to affect any major doctrine.

This is why we can say that *The Bible* is infallible as originally given. Since God and his word are infallible, we presuppose that the originals were as well.

> 6 The words of the LORD are pure words,
>
> like silver refined in a furnace on the ground,
>
> purified seven times.
>
> (Psalm 12:6)

Essential for Instruction in Faith and Practice

Not only is God's Word infallible, but it is the life-source of the Christian's faith. It is no mere *instruction manual* for life, as is so often referred as. It is the life of the Christian.

> 17 So faith comes from hearing, and hearing through the word of Christ. (Romans 10:17)

Our faith in Christ comes through the power of the word concerning Jesus. This is why our statement says that it is "essential for instruction in faith…" *The Word of God* instructs our heart to believe. Looking back at 2 Timothy, we see that Paul instructs us about the essentiality of *The Word of God*, as it pertains to Christian faith.

> 16 All Scripture is breathed out by God and profitable for teaching, for reproof, for correction, and for training in righteousness, that the man of God may be complete, equipped for every good work. (2 Timothy 3:16)

We see the essential nature of *Scripture* in the words "profitable for teaching…" The word "sufficiency" is often used to describe this essential nature—meaning that all that we need to know about God, and living a life of faith in him, is contained in this book. And the aim of such instruction is that it would "complete" the man of God in "every good work." Two things are worth mentioning about this verse as it pertains to the Christian.

Selective Hearing

First, we should notice the word "all". As argued earlier, it's not only human to error, but it's also human to select what we hear. This is an innate quality of human beings, and we need not look further than the toddler to prove it.

For example, I've often announced with the greatest urgency, "Kids, pick up your toys!" only to be met with no recognition of my existence. But as soon as I give the slightest whisper, "Ice cream's here," all the kids gather around the table from the four corners of the earth in the blink of an eye like it's the second coming of Jesus.

Obviously, they hear what they want to hear, and shut out what they don't. Now, we adults are the same way. It's just we are more sophisticated in our ignorance, and refined in our taste. We have "finer" desserts. This is especially true when it comes to spiritual taste —even for the Christian.

We love to pick and choose the parts of *The Bible* that we like, and disregard the ones we don't. We tend to distill the *Scriptures* through the filter of our own thoughts rather than distilling our thoughts through the filter of *Scripture*.

One of the reasons why we do this is because the *Scriptures* make us uncomfortable. But if we believe God's testimony about his own word, then shouldn't we learn to love and cherish the entire Bible? After all, all *Scripture* is "profitable for teaching and reproof."—for the building up of our faith in Jesus. Every time we open our Bibles— whether it's in Genesis or John, Exodus or Ephesians—God is working to strengthen our faith in Jesus and instruct us how to practice that faith in him.

So let's put away the fear of being uncomfortable with certain portions of *Scripture*. Truth will always press our conscience in uncomfortable ways, especially if we are in the presence of a holy God. It is there, in his presence, where we tremble at his strength, while tasting of his goodness.

> 11 Serve the LORD with fear,
> and rejoice with trembling.
> (Psalm 2:11)

The *Word of God* instructs us in faith—how to exercise faith— how to put legs to the truths that we behold in Christ. This is why any good preacher will always argue from *The Bible*, and let God speak for himself. He won't try and fit the triangle-shaped peg of *The Bible* into a round hole by saying what he wants it to say. He won't preach a sermon saturated with practical application and littered with a few proof texts from Proverbs. No. Rather, he will un-cage the *Word of God* and let him roar. He will let God sanctify. He will let God instruct for building up his people.

The Sufficient Revelation of Jesus

Now, the reason that the *Scriptures* are essential for instruction in faith and practice, is because they are the sufficient revelation of Jesus himself—his person and his work, as our statement says. Notice Jesus' words both about the *Scriptures* and himself and how they intersect in Luke 24.

> "44 These are my words that I spoke to you while I was still with you, that everything written about me in the Law of Moses and the Prophets and the Psalms must be fulfilled." 45 Then he opened their minds to understand the Scriptures, 46 and said to them, "Thus it is written, that the Christ should suffer and on the third day rise from the dead, 47 and that repentance and forgiveness of sins should be proclaimed in his name to all nations, beginning from Jerusalem." (Luke 24:44-47)

Jesus says that all *Scripture* is about him. Therefore we affirm that not only is all *Scripture* essential for faith and practice, but the reason it's essential is because *all of Scripture testifies of Jesus*. Wherever we turn in this book, Jesus is on the page. He is the center of every story, every law, every poem, and every prophet. As the Puritan Cotton Mather once said, "He is the key that unlocks all of the scriptures."[5] So, without *The Bible*, we do not have faith, nor practice, because we have not Christ. And without Christ, we don't have God. (John 14:6)

This, however, doesn't mean that God cannot impress upon us certain things about himself, or speak to us through those with gifts of wisdom, knowledge, or prophecy. But it does, however, mean that the finality of all we know about God is contained within Jesus. And this book, this *Bible,* is the testimony about him.

A Road to London

Charles Spurgeon once sat in a church in England, listening to a young Christian preacher give an entire sermon without ever mentioning Jesus. Afterward, Spurgeon approached the young preacher with his concern and the young man responded by saying that Jesus wasn't in the text that he preached from. And in Spurgeon-like fashion, he responded:

> "Don't you know young man that from every town, and every village, and every little hamlet in England, wherever it may be, there is a road to London?"
>
> "Yes," said the young man.
>
> "Ah!" said Spurgeon, "and so from every text in Scripture, there is a road to the metropolis of the Scriptures, that is Christ. And my dear brother, your business is when you get to a text, to say, 'Now what is the road to Christ?' and then preach a sermon, running along the road towards the great metropolis—Christ."
>
> "And," said he, "I have never yet found a text that had not got a road to Christ in it, and if I ever do find one that was not a road to Christ in it, I will make one; I will go over hedge and ditch but I would get at my Master."[6]

The Bible and its story, centers ultimately on one thing—one person—Jesus Christ the Son of God, and it is in *The Bible* that we know who he is.

Authoritative

Therefore, given all that *Scripture* says about itself—that it is inspired, infallible, essential for instruction in faith and practice, and the sufficient revelation of Christ Jesus, then it also follows that *The Bible* possesses a supreme authority. It is the final authority.

> 8 The grass withers and the flower fades,
> but the word of our God will stand forever.
> (Isaiah 40:8)

Our affirmation is punctuated with this sentence: "Therefore the Word of God is our final authority." Let's just pause here and meditate on what it means to possess authority, and moreover *final authority*.

When we think of authorities in our own contexts—parents, employers, police, landlords, etc.—we think of those who have the final say in the matters that they have jurisdiction over. We have to answer to them on their terms that they have laid out.

Parents' terms come in the form of house rules. Employers' terms come in the form of an employee handbook. Police's terms come in the form of the law. Landlords' terms come in the form of a lease agreement. All of these documents express the expectations that we must answer to, and are, in a sense, an extension of the authority itself.

The Bible operates the same way, except it's a document by which *everything* and *everyone* must answer to, because everything and everyone answers to the one who wrote the document. What this means is that what we know about reality will not ultimately come from other men, popes, priests, imams, gurus, or pastors. The final authority by which everyone must answer is God in his Word—*The Bible*. God has the final say.

How Do You Know?

This is a controversial concept, no doubt. Most people have a problem with the idea that this "antiquated book" has authority over my life in the 21st century.

> "Why would I subject myself to a book like this, when there are plenty of other books that claim to be the same. There is no way that we can know for sure that this book is from God. It seems too easy to say that *The Bible* is God's Word without any evidence for such a claim."

The idea that God's Word has authority over our lives is even hard for some Christians to accept. On the one hand, there is a part of us that whole-heartedly affirms, "Jesus loves me. This I know."

But there also might be a part that wonders, "Well how do I know?"

And the first part would answer, "Because *The Bible* tells me so."

But the other part would rebut, "Well, how do you know *The Bible* is true?"

And the first part would conclude—possibly unsatisfactory —"Because *The Bible* says that *The Bible* is true."

Wow! How convenient, and anti-climactic, right? But this doesn't have to be an unsatisfactory answer. What if I were to demonstrate that every worldview has this same predicament.

The Atheist Dilemma

Take the atheist for instance (because they seem to be the biggest anti-faith proponent). The atheist would likely have a problem with Christians saying, "*The Bible* is true because *The Bible* says so." They would recognize this as the logical "fallacy" of circular reasoning, or "begging the question" (*petitio principii*).

But the problem with this accusation is that the atheist fails to recognize he is in the same boat. He, too, is begging the question, only from a different premise. How so?

The atheist would affirm, "I start with evidence!" But does he really? I would argue that the atheist, too, must begin with an ultimate faith commitment.

If Bill Nye was to say, "I use facts and reason to determine what is true. I don't need to believe in something in which there is absolutely no evidence."

Then I would reply, "Can you give me a reason why you believe that?"

Now, the moment he says, "Because…" he has revealed his ultimate faith commitment. He has apparently just argued *petitio principii*. He has argued for *reason* using *reason*. He is stuck in a predicament he himself has created. He can't prove that reason is true apart from using reason. This is as deep as he can go with evidence.

Bill Nye and the likes will try to get us to believe that we're crazy for not having facts and only faith, when he himself is ultimately standing on faith as well.

These are called presuppositions and everyone has them. Everyone presupposes certain truths before they come to any conclusions based on reason. So then, what does this have to do with *The Bible* being authoritative?

The Authority of Scripture and Reason

This goes back to question, "How do we know *The Bible* is true?" We answer with no qualms, "Because *The Bible* says it's true…" We can confidently affirm this because *The Bible* answers to no higher authority. As the old hymn by William Cowper says, "God is his own interpreter…"

Reason, logic, evidences, and any other part of his creation, though wonderful and good, can never authenticate God. They can only confirm him. They cannot have the final say on truth because all truths are contained in him. And we can take great comfort in this. Our God is the final authority and his Word alone has the final say over our lives.

30 The word of the LORD proves true.

(Psalm 18:30)

Pillar 1 Endnotes

[1] The terms "Bible", "Word of God", and "Scripture" will all be used interchangeably.

[2] The word "Apostle" here refers to those twelve men who witnessed the risen Christ, were chosen by the Holy Spirit to preach the gospel, and performed signs and wonders that confirmed their message.

[3] You can find this debate on Apologetics 315 website. **http:// www.apologetics315.com/media/wilson-barker-debate.mp3**

[4] It's estimated that to date we have 5,800 Greek manuscripts and 10,000 Latin manuscripts.

[5] Cotton Mather, *Addresses to Old Men, and Young Men, and Little Children* (Boston: R. Pierce for Nicholas Buttolph, 1690), 9-10.

[6] Charles Spurgeon Christ Precious to Believers: Sermon 222 preached on March 13, 1859.

Pillar 2
God

Affirmation

Regarding God's nature, we believe in one God [1]—eternal [2], living [3], holy [4], true [5], and all-glorious [6], existing in three distinct persons, while sharing divine perfection in their one essence, [7] comprising of the Father [8], the Son [9], and the Holy Spirit [10].

[1] Deuteronomy 6:4; [2] Genesis 1:1; [3] Matthew 16:16; [4] Isaiah 6:3;
[5] Romans 3:4; [6] Psalm 138:5; [7] John 17:21; Matthew 18:19; [8] Malachi 2:10;
[9] John 1:1; 5:18; [10] John 15:26

As to God's divine perfection, we believe He is unchanging [1], boundless in knowledge [2], infinite in power [3], limitless in His presence[4], perfect in His wisdom [5], justice [6], mercy, grace, faithfulness, and love [7].

[1] Numbers 23:19; [2] Isaiah 46:9-10; [3] Jeremiah 32:17; [4] Jeremiah 23:24;
[5] Romans 11:33; [6] Deuteronomy 32:4; [7] Exodus 34:6

As to God's character, we believe that God has revealed himself truly [1], though not exhaustively [2], in His creation [3], in the human conscience [4], and by divine revelation through His Word—*The Bible*. In so doing, He has displayed His regard for His creatures [5].

[1] Hebrews 1:1-3; [2] Romans 11:33-36; [3] Romans 1:17; [4] Romans 2:15; [5] Hebrews 1:1-2

As to God's work, we believe the Father, Son, and Holy Spirit share in the work of creation [1], providential governance [2], judgment [3], and salvation [4].

[1] Genesis 1:1, 26, Psalm 33:6; [2] Romans 11:33-36; [3] Acts 10:42; [4] Psalm 34:22

God's Nature

We have divided this portion of our *Affirmation of Faith* into three parts: 1) God's nature, 2) his character in his communication, and 3) his work. Let's begin with God's nature. What makes God, God? The theological term behind this question is: What is God's *ontology*? What does God's *ontological* nature consist of?

God is One

The Israelites considered Deuteronomy 6:4 to be the summary of the entire Old Testament Law, and the greatest commandment given. Jesus himself made this same assertion. (Mark 12:29-31) It was referred to as the *shema* in Hebrew. It reads:

> 4 Hear, O Israel: The LORD our God, the LORD is one. (Deuteronomy 6:4)

The greatest command in all of Scripture, even affirmed by Jesus, began with a statement on God's nature. God is one. At the height of the Old Testament Scripture is the affirmation of God's one-ness. And lest we think that this may have been lost in the New Testament, we see this drawn out in James as well.

> 19 You believe that *God is one*; you do well. Even the demons believe—and shudder! (James 2:19)

So our affirmation on God begins with the radical notion that there is only one God. There are no other gods. This assertion was revolutionary and unlike any other belief throughout history—unlike the Babylonians, the Philistine, the Greeks, or Romans, who all had their plethora of gods to choose from. This belief is even unlike many religions of today in Hinduism, spiritualism, or Mormonism. *There is one God* just as there has always been—just as there will always be.

The implication of God's one-ness means that there were no other gods before him, nor will there be any gods after him. Part of what it means to be the only God, is that he is the source of all things. All things come from him alone, and nothing came before him. The word that we have chosen to describe this aspect of God's nature is "eternal".

Eternal

When we open *The Bible* and read the first few words in Genesis 1:1 we are met with this eternal God. "In the beginning, God…" As long as there has been a beginning to the world, there has also been God. The Psalms also celebrate this aspect of his nature.

> 2 Before the mountains were brought forth,
> or ever you had formed the earth and the world,
> from everlasting to everlasting you are God.
> (Psalm 90:2)

The idea of an eternal being can be a stumbling block for many because the idea of something existing forever is unfathomable. Humans have nothing to compare him with. How can something, let alone someone, always be? We would prefer to worship something that we could understand better—perhaps something finite we could grasp with our mind, or make with our hands.

Humanity's Hurdle

Idolatry has been the bane of human existence. Human beings are prone to fashion gods in the image of things created—in things understood—in things like ourselves. This is the idolatry of our day.

We love to worship ourselves. It's not uncommon for us to believe in a god that thinks and feels exactly the way we do. We tend to define God rather than letting him define us. It's funny how much God looks a lot like me when I do this.

Fashioning an image of God is appealing to us because it can both give us a sense of spiritualism while also never demanding that we bend a little, let alone break. We imagine him to be finite, like we are. We make him more comprehendible so as to sleep better at night. In the end, this god is simply not that great, and we are okay with that. But the God of *The Bible* has something to say to that—something about his ontological nature.

14 "I AM WHO I AM."

(Exodus 3:14)

The God who created the world and all that is within it had decided to reveal himself to a Hebrew man named Moses. And when Moses asked,

> "If I come to the people of Israel and say to them, 'The God of your fathers has sent me to you,' and they ask me, 'What is his name?' what shall I say to them?" God…said, "Say this to the people of Israel, 'I AM has sent me to you.'" (Exodus 3:13-14)

The true God is not defined by anything or anyone, because he is "I AM." God could have said, "I *was* this God" or "I *will be* this God", but he rather chooses the self-sustaining, self-existent designation in the present verb "I AM." He simply is, as he always was, as he will always be, unchanging and eternal.

The Living God

Our statement continues by affirming what may already be obvious. If God is eternal, and if his name is "I AM", then it follows that he too is "living". But "living" means more than just mere existence.

When Jesus turned to Simon Peter and asked him, "Who do you say that I am?" Peter replied, "You are the Christ, the Son of the *living* God." (Matthew 16:16)

So what does it mean to be "living"? Let's begin by thinking of what it means to be dead. When we look at a corpse, we see a mere shell. There is no animation, no activity, no involvement, no warmth, no laughter, and no tears. It's just cold skin, bone, and lifeless matter.

Now, let's think of death's opposite. What is life? Life is warm. It's animated. Life contains laughter and tears, mourning and rejoicing, comfort and strife. There is movement, activity, and involvement in all forms of life.

That is what it means for God to be living. He is living and he is working. He is moving and active, speaking and animating with his very speech. (Hebrews 1:3) All the life and color that we witness in his world testifies of his living nature. He's not a god who dies like Balder in Norse mythology. He cannot die.

God is Holy

We continue by affirming that God is not only living, but holy. When Isaiah is describing his vision, he sees angels ascribing to God this unique attribute.

3 And one called to another and said:
"Holy, holy, holy is the LORD of hosts;
the whole earth is full of his glory!"
(Isaiah 6:3)

Isaiah describes these angelic beings ascribing holiness to God three times. God is three-times holy, meaning that he is the essence of moral perfection. He is completely set apart in his virtue and character. He is not just one time holy, which would be a sufficient holiness in itself. God is the complete paradigm for holiness. Another way to describe God's three-times holiness is to say that he is *infinitely* holy. There are no bounds to his moral perfection.

God is True

Not only is God holy, but also he is true. There is no lie in him. When Paul writes to the Romans he anticipates counterarguments that want to exalt mankind to a distinguished position of truth. But Paul quickly extinguishes that thought.

> 3 What if some were unfaithful? Does their faithlessness nullify the faithfulness of God? 4 By no means! *Let God be true though every one were a liar...* (Romans 3:3-4)

The context of Romans 3:3-4 is that some Jews in Rome doubted that God would fulfill his promises. (Cf. also Romans 9:6) There were concerns that God either wasn't willing to deliver on his promises, or he was unable.

Paul is quick to respond. "Let God be true, and everyone a liar." The point is that God cannot break his word. It's an impossibility in the purest sense. There is no deceit in God. (Isaiah 53:9) There is no double-talk. (Numbers 23:19) Everything he promises, he delivers, and it's in this that we see that his true-ness is intricately tied to his holiness.

Now up to this point, we have only observed the intrinsic attributes of God—his ontology, so to speak. But let's now turn our attention from God's intrinsic nature to the display of that nature. How do his inward attributes emanate outward?

Yes, God is pleased with his intrinsic nature and he delights in himself. But he also delights in displaying himself—in making his intrinsic worth known. The word used to describe this is "glory."

God is All Glorious

God is glorious and he loves his own glory. Our statement says this very thing. "He is all glorious."

4 All the kings of the earth shall give you thanks, O LORD,
    for they have heard the words of your mouth,
    and they shall sing of the ways of the LORD,
        for great is the *glory* of the LORD.
(Psalm 138:4)

"Great is the glory of the LORD." If we combine all of his intrinsic attributes—his one-ness, eternality, living nature, infinite holiness, and trueness—we will discover in his word that he takes pleasure in displaying them for the cosmos to behold. This is the glory of God. As the very nature of the sun is to shine, so it is the nature of God to emanate his manifold perfections as Father, Son, and Holy Spirit.

The Holy Trinity

Now, we conclude this first portion of our affirmation of God's nature with a peculiar statement about how his nature exists within himself—that God exists in "three distinct persons, while sharing divine perfection in their one essence."

God, in his one-ness, now exists, just as he always has and always will, in three distinct persons—The Father, the Son, and the Holy Spirit. (Our third, fourth, and fifth pillars are devoted to each of these persons).

Throughout history the Church has designated this concept as *The Trinity*. *The Bible* testifies to the existence of all three, while affirming also the one-ness of God. The following is a small sample of the verses that pertain to both the one-ness of God, and the plurality within him.[1]

The Father

> 10 Have we not all *one* Father? Has not *one* God created us? Why then are we faithless to one another, profaning the covenant of our fathers? (Malachi 2:10)

The Son

> 1 In the beginning was the Word, and the Word was with God, and *the Word was God*...14 And *the Word became flesh and dwelt among us,* and we have seen his glory, glory as of *the only Son from the Father,* full of grace and truth. (John 1:1, 14)

The Holy Spirit

> "26 But when the Helper comes, whom I will send to you from the Father, *the Spirit* of truth, who *proceeds from the Father*, he will bear witness about me." (John 15:26)

What we find in these scriptures is the distinct personhood of all three. All three have differences between them. The Son is not the Father, and the Father is not the Son, and neither are the Spirit, nor the Spirit either one of them. Yet, at the same time, they each possess the fullness of deity, meaning that they are co-identical in nature and co-equal in glory. The tendency, usually at this point, is to think that they are each a part of God. Some have used an egg as an analogy for the Trinitarian God-head. But the problem with this analogy is that an egg is made up of a shell, yolk, and egg white. They are three different parts to the whole.

Scripture is careful to not assert this. "For in him [Jesus] the *fullness of deity* dwells bodily." (Colossians 2:9) The three distinct persons *share* in the whole perfection and essence of the one God.

Now, at this point, I imagine some of our brains might be feeling a bit stretched, like our mind is being drawn and quartered. So let me explain how God's Trinitarian nature is even possible.

Making Sense of the Trinity

Even though each person in God is not the other, at the same time, they mutually indwell one another while still preserving their differences. The Father is not the Son, but the Father is wholly *in* the Son, and the same goes with the Holy Spirit.

There is a word to describe this very thing.[2] The early church fathers recognized this concept, and created in the fourth century the word *perichoresis*. Perichoresis is the mutual indwelling of the three persons of the Trinity.[3]

Jesus' High Priestly prayer in John 17 is a classic demonstration of God's perichoretic nature. Jesus prays:

"20 I do not ask for these only, but also for those who will believe in me through their word, 21 that they may all be one, *just as you, Father, are in me, and I in you*, that they also may be in us, so that the world may believe that you have sent me. 22 The glory that you have given me I have given to them, that they may be one even as we are one, 23 I in them and *you in me*, that they may become perfectly one." (John 17:20-23)

Jesus prays to the Father. He does not pray to himself. Jesus is not the Father, but he is *in* the Father and the Father is in him. God's perichoretic nature simply means that each person within God is distinct from one another, yet mutually indwelling one another.

Hard on the Brain

If this is a hard concept to grasp, we actually should be oddly encouraged by that. After all, a god that we can fully comprehend is not a god worth worshiping. Furthermore, it follows that an infinite God is not to be fully understood by finite minds. We should expect that some things are not intended to be understand about God in their entirety.

29 The secret things belong to the LORD our God, but the things that are revealed belong to us and to our children forever… (Deuteronomy 29:29)

So, we shouldn't be surprised that our three pounds of nervous tissue floating in our three pound skull would have a hard time comprehending the complexities of the God who holds the galaxies in his hand. But rather, our souls should be encouraged by the grandeur of God as we revel in his magnanimous beauty and complexity. After all, infinite perfection will be a beauty that will take eternity to revel in.

Divine Perfection

We also affirm with God's Trinitarian nature that he is also unchanging in nature. Our statement reads, "As to God's divine perfection, we believe He is unchanging…"

Part of the perfection of the triune God is that he doesn't change. He is not a wishy-washy, shape-shifter. He actually would make a terrible politician in this way.

> 19 God is not a man that he should lie,
> Nor a son of man, that he should change his mind.
> (Leviticus 23:19)

God doesn't change. He is true all the time. He's never inconsistent in his speech, conduct, or character. He is, just as he always was, and as he always will be. The author of Hebrews affirms this as well when he says that God is the same "yesterday, today, and forever." (Hebrews 13:8)

Omniscient Omnipotent Omnipresent

Partnered with God's unchanging nature is his infinite knowledge, power, and presence. God is "boundless in knowledge, infinite in power, and limitless in His presence." The traditional terms for these attributes are *omniscience*, *omnipotence*, and *omnipresence*. God knows everything. God can do anything. God is everywhere.

Additional Attributes

While these three attributes speak to God's ability—the scope of his knowledge, power, and presence—the rest of our statement focuses on his inward attributes as they directly relate to us. Our statement says that God is "perfect in His wisdom, justice, mercy, grace, faithfulness, and love."

God is perfect in his *wisdom*. (Romans 11:33) We are even told in the New Testament that Jesus is the wisdom of God—he is the embodiment of God's order. (1 Corinthians 1:24)

God is also perfect in executing *justice*—always working toward what is right, upholding what is good by condemning what is evil.

At the same time we also see that God "does not deal with us according to our sin," (Psalm 103:10) hence his *mercy*. We'll look at this more carefully in the pillar on *Humanity and Its Destiny*, but for now we can at least recognize that God does not execute his justice on us now, even though we deserve it. He mercifully causes the rain to fall on both "the just and the unjust." (Matthew 5:45)

On the flip side, God continually gives us good things, which we don't deserve. This is his *grace*—a common grace extended to all and a unique grace to his children. Though his children often wander and flirt with other gods, he remains to extends his grace, and is *faithful* to meet us in his grace. And he does all of this because he *loves* us. God is loving.

God's Know-ability

The third portion of our affirmation focuses on the characteristic of God's know-ability. We affirm that God "has revealed himself truly, though not exhaustively..."

What this means is that God has shown us himself in a way that is perfectly accurate (Hebrews 1:1-3), yet he hasn't shown us himself in his entirety. (Romans 11:33-36) After all, if God is infinite in his divine perfections, how can we expect our small minds to comprehend that level of greatness?

But the fact remains that we can understand him truly and accurately because he has revealed himself. He has done this in two ways, as our affirmation states.

God Communicates in His Creation

God communicates in his creation. Paul argues in Romans 1:

19 For what can *be known* about God is plain to them, because God has shown it to them. 20 For his invisible attributes, namely, his eternal power and divine nature, have been clearly perceived, ever since the creation of the world, *in the things that have been made*. (Romans 1:19-20)

God has made the world in such a way that his fingerprints are everywhere in all the stuff that he has made. Moreover, we, as his image-bearers, have the ability to recognize him in those things, and in a limited way, to know him in them.[4]

God, in this very moment, is holding every molecule, atom, and cell together. He is sustaining every rock, bird, river, and tree by the word of his power. (Hebrews 1:3) The sun and moon are in their destined positions because he directs them. And because he is the artist behind all these masterpieces in the universe, all the masterpieces are speaking of its Artist.

God tells us about his love and care in the pinions of eagles (Psalm 91:4), his righteous reign in the lions of the Serengeti (Isaiah 31:4), his protective nature in large castles and buildings (Proverbs 18:10), his care and discipline in earthly fathers (Hebrews 12:7), his faithfulness in husbands and wives (Ephesians 5:31-32), the strength of his word in the trees planted by rivers (Psalm 1:3), his wisdom in honeycombs (Proverbs 24:13-14), and his diligence in colonies of ants (Proverbs 6:6). God is speaking in his world, because his world is packed with himself.

God Communicates in the Conscience

In addition to God's creation in nature, God also communicates to humanity by the moral center of our heart—the conscience—the "small voice" in that distinguishes right from wrong.

15 They show that the work of the law is written on their hearts, while *their conscience also bears witness*, and their conflicting thoughts accuse or even excuse them. (Romans 2:15)

The law referred to in this passage is God's law—the highest moral standard. Paul says that our consciences bear witness to this standard. Our thoughts accuse us when we lie, steal, or murder. The fact that we have a conscience is telling of our creator—that we are indeed made in his image. When we live outside the bounds of what he's created us to live within, we hear his "voice". We feel a peculiar conviction. God is speaking to us about who he is and who he isn't, and who he has made us to be.

God Communicates in His Word

However, these are not the only ways God speaks. Our statement also says that we can know God "by divine revelation through His word—*The Bible.*" Hebrews 1:1-2 says,

> 1 Long ago, at many times and in many ways, God spoke to our fathers by the prophets, 2 but in these last days he has spoken to us by his Son… (Hebrews 1:1-2)

While it's true that we can stand on the edge of the Grand Canyon and know something about God—possessing a sense of the divine (*sensus divinitatus*)[5] and unknowingly recognizing his truths—at the same time we deny and suppress this knowledge. (Romans 1:18-23)

So, God provided another way for us to know him. He spoke in words—words that we could understand. As already observed in the first pillar, we saw that God spoke through men—but particularly, and most clearly, God spoke through one man. He is the very *Word of God* —Jesus the Christ, the revelation of the infinite God. (John 13:20)

God's Character in Communication

What does God's know-ability say about God's character? After all, this whole statement begins with "Regarding *his character*". What do God's *know-ability* and his *character* have to do with one another?

In making himself known in these ways, we recognize that God has a desire for his creatures to know him. This is why we say, "He has displayed His regard for His creatures."

God has never owed it to anyone to reveal himself in any way. But because of God's nature—because of his affection for his creatures who are made in his image, he has delighted to communicate to us about himself.

We often lose sight of this. We commonly think God is distant, unattached, and indifferent to our wants, desires, and actions. We doubt that he does in fact care about what we do with our life. He cares about how we spend our time, energy, and money. We can easily slip into a view of God as only transcendent—meaning that God is really high up in the universe and cares little of what I do. And while it is true that God is *transcendent*, we affirm that he is also *immanent*. God is near. We know his nearness because we hear him speaking to us.

God's communication is telling of his regard for his creatures. He is not a god who keeps quiet, nor does he leave his creatures to figure everything out, especially by ourselves. No. He is both transcendent and immanent, speaking all the time to his creatures.

God's Work

This last portion of our affirmation focuses on God's actions. What is God doing?

"As to God's work, we believe the Father, Son, and Holy Spirit share in the work of creation, providential governance, judgment, and salvation."

While we will spend a good amount of time on the nature and work of each person in the Godhead in the subsequent pillars, we want to make it clear here that these three persons in their one essence, share the same work, though they execute different roles. So what is the work that they share?

Creation

We believe that the triune God is active in *creation*. Genesis 1:1 says, "In the beginning, God *created* the heavens and earth." The triune God is the originator and creator of everything that has been made and he has done so *ex nihilo*—out of nothing. (John 1:3)

Furthermore, God holds everything in place. All matter, in this moment, is dependent on his command. (Hebrews 1:3)

Providential Governance

In addition to God's creative work, we also believe that he providentially governs the world that he has made. God is actively, in all aspects of creation, moving it for his purposes.

"9 I am God, and there is no other;
I am God, and there is none like me,
10 declaring the end from the beginning
and from ancient times things not yet done,
saying, 'My counsel shall stand,

and I will accomplish all my purpose,'"

(Isaiah 46:9-10)

God has plans and purposes and none of those plans are interrupted. (Job 42:2) God accomplishes all that he sets out to do.

Judgment

Then there is judgment. We believe that God is actively judging now, and, one day, will judge every single person at the closing of history.

42 And he commanded us to preach to the people and to testify that he is the one appointed by God to be judge of the living and the dead. (Acts 10:42)

Being that God is morally perfect, part of his work is to judge both in the present and in the future.

In the present, God has already cast his judgment. "None is righteous. No not one." (Romans 3:10) Yet God's wrath doesn't fall on everyone. Presently, God provides salvation and shelter from his wrath for those who "36 …believe the Son. But whoever does not obey the Son has not life, but *the wrath of God remains on him.*" (John 3:36) This is the present active wrath of God.

But there is also a future wrath of God—one more intense and final. Paul says in Romans 2 that God will one day cast a judgment on humanity.

5 But because of your hard and impenitent heart you are storing up wrath for yourself *on the day of wrath* when God's righteous judgment *will* be revealed. 6 He *will* render to each one according to his works: 7 to those who by patience in well-doing seek for glory and honor and immortality, he *will* give eternal life; (Romans 2:5-7)

Notice the future tense verbs. Judgment "will be revealed." God "will render to". God "will give eternal life." God has not forgotten nor chosen to be uninvolved in his world. He cares about evil and pain. He cares about wrongdoing and suffering by evil men. I know that at times—especially when we read the world news—it may seem that everything is going crooked and God is indifferent to injustice. But we have his promises in Scripture that he will indeed carry out judgment and right every wrong there ever was.

> 4 Let the nations be glad and sing for joy,
> for you judge the peoples with equity
> and guide the nations upon earth.
> (Psalm 67:4)

So, while there is a present reality of God's active judgment, we also see that there is a more severe and urgent judgment that awaits everyone…well, not everyone.

Salvation

Our statement moves from judgment to salvation because *The Bible* also teaches that some escape this severe judgment. As deserving of God's judgment as we are, because of his mercy and grace, God provided an escape from it.

> 30…those whom he predestined he also called, and those whom he called he also justified, and those whom he justified he also glorified. (Romans 8:30)

This is God's saving work.

> 22 The LORD redeems the life of his servants;
> none of those who take refuge in him will be condemned.
> (Psalm 34:22)

> Our God is a god who delights to save. His work, from beginning to end, is a work of salvation for his people.
> 9 The Lord is not slow to fulfill his promise as some count slowness, but is patient toward you, not wishing that any should perish, but that all should reach repentance. (2 Peter 3:9)

We see in this text that before the foundations of the earth were ever laid, God was planning his great salvation. He was, from eternity, forming a blueprint to rescue his children from the perils of evil and death. (Ephesians 1:4-5)

And this is where *The Bible* climaxes—the salvation of God's people. This is the reason God created his world. History is a story of God's salvation. His pen? His spoken words—speaking into existence all matter, putting it in motion, animating his story toward the breathtaking climax—where his own Son would take his last breath, being nailed to a cross as a ransom price to buy back his people, thus rescuing them from judgment of sin and death, and ushering them into eternal life.

Behold our God—perfect in essence, loving in his speech, glorious in his character, and wonderful in his salvation.

Pillar 2 Endnotes

[1] Of course there are a number of verses that speak to each distinct person within God that you can find referenced in the statements at the beginning of the chapter.

[2] Whenever new concepts are introduced, new words are created to communicate those concepts. For example, the Christian Church has created a number of terms to describe the nature of God—words like: Trinity, omniscience, and hypostatic are just to name a few. While none of these words are in *The Bible*, all are taught in *The Bible*.

[3] Joe Rigney has a wonderful portion in his book *The Things of Earth* that addresses perichoresis. Joe Rigney, *The Things of Earth: Treasuring God by Enjoying His Gifts* (Wheaton, Illinois: Crossway, 2015), p. 37-39.

[4] We will discuss later the inability of man to comprehend God's message in creation apart from the saving work of Jesus and the new birth by the Holy Spirit.

[5] Jean Calvin, *Institutes of the Christian Religion* (Westminster: John Knox Press, U.S)

Pillar 3
God the Father

Affirmation

Regarding God the Father's nature, we believe He is an eternal, personal spirit [1] and the source of all authority.[2]

[1] John 6:46; [2] Matthew 28:18

As to God the Father's work in creation, we believe that by His decree, He created all things.

Genesis 1:1; 1 Corinthians 8:6

As to God the Father's work in redemption, we believe that by His decree He has purchased a people and adopted them as his children out of this world, [1] to conform them to the image of His Son [2], to the praise of His glorious name. [3]

[1] Ephesians 1:3-4; [2] Romans 8:28-29; [3] Ephesians 1:11-12

God the Father

Where we explored the ontological nature of God in the previous chapter, this chapter will specifically focus on the distinct person of God the Father. Who is the God the Father?

Let's start with the term "Father." Not only in *Scripture* do we see God regularly referred to as "Father," but this is his primary title in the New Testament. Often, these two designations—*God* and *Father*—are interchangeable, especially when Jesus uses them.

Jesus will refer to God as both "Father" and "God" with no distinction between the two. One such occasion is in John's account of Jesus and the woman at the well in chapter 4. Jesus explains to her the nature of God.

> "23 But the hour is coming, and is now here, when the true worshipers will worship *the Father* in spirit and truth, for *the Father is* seeking such people to worship him. 24 *God is spirit*, and those who *worship him* must worship in spirit and truth." (John 4:23-24)

We can see here that Jesus refers to God both as "Father" in verse 23 and "God" in verse 24. The takeaway from this is that "Father" seems to be the primary title for God, especially when Jesus is talking.

Father's Nature

But the designation "Father" is preliminary. Our statement really begins with the *nature* of God the Father. As explained in the previous chapter, the person of the Father is not the same person as the Son, nor the person of the Holy Spirit. While each one is entirely God, they are different.

Regarding the Father, we first affirm that he is an "eternal, personal spirit." Going back to John 4, Jesus describes his Father this way. He says to the Samaritan woman, "God is spirit." And we know that he's referring specifically to his Father because of the previous verse. The implication is that the Father is spirit.

Now what does that mean? What is a spirit? Jesus says in Luke 24:39 that "a spirit does not have flesh and bones like I do." When we say that the Father is Spirit, we mean that he cannot be defined in human terms with regard to human flesh. He doesn't have a body—no arms, no legs, no face.[1]

There are, however, false religions that teach that the Father does in fact have a body. But here we see the contrary. The Father doesn't have flesh. He is spirit. (cf. also John 6:46)

And much like we pointed out in the last pillar, because God is spirit, it follows that he is also eternal. He is not finite, limited in space and geography like we are. He is infinite.

1 In the beginning was the Word, and the Word was *with God*, and the Word was God. 2 He was in the beginning *with God*. (John 1:1-2)

What a wonderful Trinitarian verse we have in the prologue of John's gospel. Here we have the person of Jesus referred to as "the Word" and John showing us the eternality of the Word, because the Word was always "with God"—meaning the Word was with the Father.

John follows this up by showing us that the fullness of God was in Jesus. He says, "the Word was God". He then concludes his opening statement by once again affirming the eternal fellowship of God the Father with God the Son. He says, "He was in the beginning with God." Therefore, the Father is eternal, ever-present in the beginning.

Source of All Authority

The implication of the Father's eternality is that anything that follows him must come from him. And because everything comes from him, he owns it all. Our statement says, "He is the source of all authority."

Now, to help us understand how the relationship between God's ownership fits nicely with his authority, let's look at an illustration *The Bible* gives in Romans 9.

In Romans 9, Paul uses the analogy of a potter and clay. In order for a piece of pottery to come into existence there has to be at least two things—there has to be moldable clay, and there has to be someone to mold the clay. So Paul says,

21 Has the potter no *right* over the clay, to make out of the same lump one vessel for honorable use and another for dishonorable use? (Romans 9:21)

The point here is that the creator of the pot has absolute right over his creation, the clay, to do whatever he wants with it. And so it is with the Father. Since he, the potter, is the source of all things, he also possesses authority over all things—the clay. In fact, Jesus affirms this very thing in his final words to his disciples.

"18 All authority in heaven and on earth has been given to me." (Matthew 28:18)

The "giving" that Jesus talks about is a passive verb, meaning that Jesus is not the one giving all authority to himself. He is the recipient of authority. The Father gives Jesus all authority. The Father is the one who hands the reigns over to Jesus as the Lord of heaven and earth. The Father is the source of all authority because he owns all things.

The Father's Work in Creation

Shifting now from the Father's nature, our statement moves toward his work. What does the Father do? Our statement says, "we believe that by His decree, He created all things."

We use the word "decree" to indicate the Father's authoritative nature in the work of creation. The Father is the one speaking. And it's through his speech that he creates from nothing—*ex nihilo*.

Contrary to other beliefs, we hold that in the beginning there was God, and God alone—meaning there was no matter in the beginning—nothing tangible in the universe until God spoke it into existence. He creates something *out of nothing*. We see this in the opening lines of *The Bible* in Genesis 1:1.

1 In the beginning, God created the heavens and the earth…3 and God said, "Let there be light," And there was light. (Genesis 1:1,3)

Paul expounds on this *ex nihilo* doctrine in the New Testament, showing the inner dynamics between both the Son and the Father in creation. He says in 1 Corinthians 8:6:

6 …yet for us there is one God, the Father, *from whom* are all things and *for whom* we exist, and one Lord, Jesus Christ, *through whom* are all things and through whom we exist.
(1 Corinthians 8:6)

How was everything created? The Father, the source of all authority, by his decree, spoke and things came into existence. And it's in this way that all things come *from* the Father.

The Father and Son

In this passage, however, we also witness Jesus' role in creation. The distinction between these two roles may seem a little blurred, but the nuances are important enough to note.

When the Father speaks, what comes out of his mouth? His "word". And who is given this title in the New Testament? Jesus. "In the beginning was the word." (John 1:1). What this means is that the Father decrees and the decree creates. In other words, the spoken word of God—Jesus, the Son of God—is the agency by which all things are made—"through whom all things are made."

Think of building a house. You begin with an architect who draws up the plans and blueprints and then hires a general contractor to execute the work. In this illustration one person is the *source* of the house, while the other person is the *agency* of the house. This is 1 Corinthians 8:6. The Father "by his decree, created all things." He is the architect.

The Father's Work in Redemption

Finally, we move to the final portion of our affirmation. "As to God the Father's work in redemption…"

Why do we use the word "redemption"? More of this concept will be fleshed out in the Pillar *Humanity and Salvation*, but a little discussion is appropriate here, being that this is where we introduce the term "redemption".

The primary work of God throughout *The Bible* and human history is the work of salvation, as stated previously. But God's salvation is described in much more vivid terms—that of redemption —redemption being the purchase out of slavery.

Purchased

Not only do we see God's redemptive work in delivering his people out of slavery time and time again (Joseph, Moses, the Prophets in Babylon), but we also see it most pronounced in the New Testament with Jesus and his church.

3 Blessed be the God and Father of our Lord Jesus Christ, who has blessed us in Christ with every spiritual blessing in the heavenly places, 4 even as he chose us in him before the foundation of the world, that we should be holy and blameless before him. In love 5 he predestined us for adoption as sons through Jesus Christ, according to the purpose of his will, 6 to the praise of his glorious grace, with which he has blessed us in the Beloved. 7 In him we have redemption through his blood, the forgiveness of our trespasses, according to the riches of his grace... (Ephesians 1:3-7)

We specifically see God's redeeming work in verse 7. The price to purchase his people was the currency of his Son's own blood. And this plan began with the Father "by his decree." Yes, it was executed through the agency of God the Son, in the same way that creation was executed through the Son. But the Father is the mastermind behind the redemptive plan. He is the one, who "chose us in him before the foundation of the world," (Ephesians 1:4)

Adopted

And so the Father uses the blood of Jesus as the payment to buy his people out of slavery from sin and death. But this is only half of the tale. Whenever a slave was bought out of slavery, it meant that the slave would then have a new master. So if the Father buys us out of the slavery of sin and death, *what does he buy us into*? What is the Father's plan once we're free from sin and death? Let's look at our Ephesians passage one more time, specifically at verse 5.

5 …*for* adoption as sons through Jesus Christ. (Ephesians 1:5)

The Father buys his people not to put us up in a foster home, but to bring us under his own roof, as his own—to be a part of his family—to make us sons and daughters by the blood of his Son, while we were sinners. (Romans 5:8) And just like children, we will grow into the likeness of our Father, under his roof, just as the firstborn Son is in the perfect likeness of his Father.

To Conform

Part of the Father's redemptive plan is not only to buy us and bring us into his home, as his children, but to conform us to be like his unique Son, Jesus.

29 For those whom he foreknew he also predestined to be conformed to the image of his Son, in order that he might be the firstborn among many brothers. (Romans 8:29)

It's no wonder that God is "Father". Children imitate their fathers. My children say the same words I do. They sing the same songs that I sing. They like the same sports that I like. Children are a reflection and image of their fathers. And God, as Father, has both commanded that we imitate him (Ephesians 5:1), and promised that he will work in us to make us more like him in Jesus—to conform us to his image in his Son. This is a monumental task and one that will take an eternity to complete.

The implications are that though we will always be beloved children of the Father, we will also always be in the process of conforming to the image of the Father's firstborn Son—Jesus. The word for this process is "sanctification." While we will never cease to be children of God, we will also never cease conforming to his likeness. We continue to pilgrim the road of holiness. And under our Father's guidance and discipline, he will see to it that we will become like him in Jesus—holy and righteous.

To the Glory of the Father

Our statement concludes with the glory of the Father. As the head of the Trinitarian fellowship, and the one possessing all authority, this means all glory directs toward him. In fact, the passage that we explored in Ephesians a little earlier emphasized this glory. Three times Paul states the ultimate aim of God's redeeming work.

> 6…to the praise of his glorious grace. (Ephesians 1:6)
> 12…to the praise of his glory. (Ephesians 1:12)
> 14…to the praise of his glory. (Ephesians 1:14)

The Father's nature, the Father's creative work, and the Father's redemptive work all aim at the same purpose—the glory of his name. Indeed this is the aim in all that he does.

God's End in Creation

After the Apostle Paul expounds on the sovereign grace of God being extended to the Gentiles in Romans 9-11, he ends with a worship song that sings of this same glory.

33 Oh, the depth of the riches and wisdom and knowledge of God! How unsearchable are his judgments and how inscrutable his ways!

> 34 "For who has known the mind of the Lord,
> or who has been his counselor?"
> 35 "Or who has given a gift to him
> that he might be repaid?"

36 *For from him and through him and to him are all things.* To him be glory forever. Amen. (Romans 11:33-36)

This is the end for which God created the world—that all would behold and enjoy his manifold perfections, delighting in him, and being satisfied in him forevermore.

Pillar 3 Endnotes

[1] The Bible often ascribes human attributes to God, especially in the Old Testament. He is said to have "hands" (Genesis 3:22), a face (Exodus 33:20), and a back (Exodus 33:23). These types of depictions are often referred to as "anthropomorphisms". They are ways to describe the infinite using finite things. The Psalmist says in Psalm 57:1 that he finds refuge in the shadow of God's wings. Of course this doesn't mean that the author believes God has wings. He is simply communicating, by way of comparison, an attribute of God using objects in our world that we understand. Wings communicate protection.

Pillar 4
God The Son

Affirmation

Regarding God the Son's nature, we believe that He is the Son of God[1], being of one essence with the Father [2], eternally proceeding from Him, and without beginning [3]. He was conceived in the flesh by the Holy Spirit [4], born of a virgin [5], and is both fully God and fully man. [6]

[1] John 20:31; [2] Colossians 2:9; [3] Colossians 1:15-16; John 1:1;
[4] Matthew 1:18; [5] Matthew 1:23; [6] John 6:46; 10:30, 38; Titus 2:13;
Philippians 2:6-8; Colossians 1:15-17; 2:9;
Revelation 4:11

As to God the Son's work in creation, we believe that He, as the very Word of God [1], is the agent by which all things were created [2], and are ever-sustained. [3]

[1] John 1:14; [2] John 1:3; [3] Hebrews 1:3, Colossians 1:15-17

As to God the Son's work in redemption, we believe that He lived a perfectly obedient life [1], died a substitutionary death, having been crucified on a cross to atone for our sins [2], rose bodily from the dead [3], and ascended into the heavens [4] as witnessed by many [5], where He now advocates at the right hand of the Father [6] on behalf of those who believe in Him. [7]

[1] Hebrews 4:15; [2] 1 Corinthians 15:3; [3] 1 Corinthians 15:4;
[4] Luke 24:29-43, 51-53; [5] 1 Corinthians 15:5-8; [6] 1 John 2:1;
Hebrews 7:25; [7] Romans 1:16; Ephesians 2:8-9

The Son of God

Our statement is divided into three portions—the Son's *nature*, his work in *creation*, and his work in *redemption*. But before we begin looking at his nature, let's first camp out on the designation "Son of God." Where does this title come from?

We see "Son of God" throughout *Scripture*. We especially notice this in the gospel accounts where Jesus is the revealed "Son of God" who was spoken of in the Old Testament Scriptures. (Psalm 2:7)

At the very end of John's gospel, he tells us that believing in the Son of God is the whole reason he penned this gospel.

> 31…but these are written so that you may believe that Jesus is the Christ, *the Son of God*, and that by believing you may have life in his name." (John 20:31)

When John writes his historical account of Jesus' life, death, and resurrection he does so with the aim that the reader would not only believe that Jesus is the Messiah, but also that he would believe that Jesus is the Son of God.

This is why our statement begins with Jesus as the Son of God. The entirety of *Scripture* speaks of him in this way. But what does it mean to be the Son of God? Let's look more closely at the nature of God the Son.

Being of One Essence

Our affirmation says that the Son of God is "…of one essence with the Father…" Now if we pause and think about our own lives, and what makes us "us", then we can similarly see that we share the essence of our fathers and mothers. How? We look like them. We take on their characteristics. We walk like them. We stand like them. We share their voice and vocabulary. We are each a product of the merging essences of both our moms and dads.

Jesus is the same, except that he shares the entirety of the essence with his Father. Colossians 2:9 says that the "fullness of deity dwells bodily" with Jesus, meaning that there is not any portion of God the Son that is not God. Jesus shares the divine essence with his Father.

Now, we must be clear here. Jesus is not a *part* of God, like a shell is part of an egg (as we saw in the previous pillar). Rather, the fullness of God's divinity resides within his Son. Remember *perichoresis*? The author of Hebrews reminds us of the fullness of the Son's deity when he specifically says, "He is the radiance of the glory of God and the *exact* imprint of his nature…" (Hebrews 1:3) Jesus is not a part of God. He is the "exact" imprint of his nature, thus he is "of one essence."

To be clear, we must again remember that although the Father and Son share the same divine essence, they are not the same. They are different persons who *function* differently in their relationship with one another.

For example, as we have seen, God is the *originator* of creation, yet, at the same time, the *means* by which he creates is through his Son. The point being, that although they are one, they are not the identical persons. They are distinct. The Son is not the Father, but the Son comes from the Father.

Eternally Proceeding From the Father

To be the "Son of God" means that Jesus shares the divine nature of his Father in one essence, yet he proceeds from his Father—like a child proceeds from his parents. This is why our statement reads that Jesus is "eternally proceeding from Him [the Father], and without beginning."

However, we should pause right here and make a distinction between earthly children and parents, and the divine Father and Son, because they are not the same. The analogy breaks down at this point.

While the Son of God comes from the Father, much like an earthly son comes after his father, the comparison is not entirely the same. Earthly sons have a beginning, but Jesus never did. The Father, the Son, and the Holy Spirit were never created. Neither of them had an origin. They all are the original.

As human beings, we might struggle with this. We don't have a reference point for eternality. We are finite mortal beings. We have a birth and we have a death. We have a beginning and an end. There is a distinct point in time and history that we all come into existence.

But when we look at the eternal Godhead, not one of them had a beginning. They are all equally eternal, neither having an origin. This is why we can have scriptures that both show Jesus' nature as "firstborn" *and* his eternality. Let's look at Colossians 1:15.

15 He is the image of the invisible God, the *firstborn of all creation*. (Colossians 1:15)

Our statement says that the Son of God "eternally proceeds from the Father" because of verses like Colossians 1:15. He has, and always will proceed from the Father.

Without Beginning

As stated above, this can certainly put a strain on our finite mind…and it should. If we were to completely understand God, then he would prove to be no god at all—just a small god made in our own image. Trying to understand the infinite *should* stretch both our hearts and minds. At the same time, this doesn't mean we can't strive for more understanding.

I'm appreciative of the saints in our history who have labored to understand the deep things of God and communicate them in a way that we can understand him and so worship him more dearly. Saints like Jonathan Edwards have labored in understanding God and have helped us better understand complex things like the Trinity. Particularly, Edwards wrote a short essay that helped explain better the relationship between the Father, Son and Holy Spirit.

In this work, Edwards was able to demonstrate God's eternal thought-life of himself. What he demonstrated in *Scripture* was that God always had an idea of himself—or a thought—an internal word. And in thinking of himself, he was able to see himself perfectly. Like we have an image in our head of who we are, God does as well. But unlike us, his picture is perfectly accurate. And since God is eternal, he always had this picture of himself—this thought of himself. We could say that it was an eternal self-image—an inward thought powerful enough that it is a person.[1] We see this idea come from scriptures like John 1:1.

> 1 In the beginning was the Word, and the Word was with God, and the Word was God. (John 1:1)

The point here is that Jesus is the very thought of God—the internal word from the Father that he always had of himself. As long as God the Father was thinking, which is from eternity, he always had an eternal idea of himself—a word concerning who he was. And that word was Jesus.

That may be one way we can understand this relationship between the Father and Son, and it may be a stretch for some. But the point stands. Jesus is "without beginning".

The three are, and always have been, an eternal society in continual communion with one another. But this community would undergo a radical change at the incarnation of the Son of God, which leads us to our next portion in the affirmation. It states:

"He was conceived in the flesh by the Holy Spirit, born of a virgin, and is both fully God and fully man."

Conceived in the Flesh

Unlike the many denials of the Trinity,[2] we hold to the traditional belief that Jesus is the Son of God, being equal with the Father, while maintaining his humanity.

As a man, Jesus entered his world just as all men do—through the birth of a woman. We don't believe that Jesus appeared out of the sky, nor that he arose up out of the primordial waters. Rather, Jesus was born in the same way that all men are born—from a woman— except he was born from a virgin woman. Matthew 1:18 and verse 23 reads:

> 18 Now the birth of Jesus Christ took place in this way. When his mother Mary had been betrothed to Joseph, before they came together she was found to be with child from the Holy Spirit... 23 "Behold, the virgin shall conceive and bear a son, and they shall call his name Immanuel" (which means, God with us)." (Matthew 1:18, 23)

The historical account of Matthew shows us that Mary was pregnant with Jesus. The angel of God then informs Mary that the conception was by the Holy Spirit and not by a man, thus Jesus would possess both the full nature of man (Mary) and the full nature of God (the Holy Spirit).

Fully God and Fully Man

The term that the historic Church created to describe the full nature of God and man in Jesus is referred to as the *hypostatic union*. Jesus is simultaneously both God and man. "For in him the fullness of deity dwells bodily." (Colossians 2:9)

John, the evangelist, also demonstrates this union of mortal and divine in his gospel in John 10:38. He records Jesus saying,

> "but if I do [the works], even though you do not believe me, believe the works, that you may know and understand that *the Father is in me and I am in the Father.*" (John 10:38)

This isn't the only place Jesus speaks this way. In an ever-escalating argument with the Pharisees in John 8, Jesus climaxes the debate by appealing to the union between him and his Father. John records Jesus saying,

> 56 "Your father Abraham rejoiced that he would see my day. He saw it and was glad."
>
> 57 So the Jews said to him, "You are not yet fifty years old, and have you seen Abraham?"
>
> 58 Jesus said to them, "Truly, truly, I say to you, before Abraham was, *I am.*" (John 8:56-58)

What a remarkable claim. Jesus claimed deity when he said, "I Am"—which the Pharisees and scribes would have immediately recognized from Moses' account in Exodus. Jesus thought of himself as equal with God the Father, though he himself was in human form. (Philippians 2:6-7)

So the eternality, deity, and humanity of Jesus are all the things that make up his nature. Let's now examine his work. What did Jesus do and what is he now doing?

The Son is the Word and Agent of Creation

Our statement says:

"As to God the Son's work in creation, we believe that He, as the very Word of God, is the agent by which all things were created, and are ever-sustained."

As we have already seen, the Father is the "originator" of creation while Jesus is the one who executes the creative work—like the architect/contractor analogy. The Son of God is the means by which God the Father's world becomes tangible.

3 All things were made through him, and without him was not any thing made that was made. (John 1:3)

3 He is the radiance of the glory of God and the exact imprint of his nature, and he upholds the universe by the word of his power. (Hebrews 1:3)

In both texts we see that Jesus is the *agency* of God's work in creating and sustaining our world. He is the creator and sustainer of all matter—of all atoms, protons, electrons, neutrons, cells, mitochondria, chromosomes, DNA, molecules, hydrogen, nitrogen, oxygen, water, rocks, dirt, mountains, trees, clouds, sky, atmosphere, sun, planets, stars, solar systems, and galaxies. "All things were made *through* him…" (John 1:3) "…he upholds the universe *by* the word of his power." (Hebrews 1:3)

If we look at Colossians 1:15-16 we see that this passage, while addressing the eternal nature of Jesus, also affirms his work in creation the same way.

> "15 [Jesus] is the image of the invisible God, the firstborn of all creation. 16 For *by* him all things were created, in heaven and on earth, visible and invisible, whether thrones or dominions or rulers or authorities—all things were created through him and for him."[3] (Colossians 1:15-16)

In this very moment that you are reading this paragraph, God, in Jesus, is working. He is holding all of existence together. The reason the sun came up this morning is because Jesus commanded it.

Creation, however, is not the only work of God the Son. It is an important work, but it isn't the work that God delights in the most. In fact, the reason for his incarnation—his becoming a man—was for the purpose of redeeming his creation and moreover, saving his people for the glory of his own name. Our statement reads:

"As to God the Son's work in redemption, we believe that He lived a perfectly obedient life, died a substitutionary death, having been crucified on a cross to atone for our sin…"

God the Son and Redemption

We already spent some time on the word "redemption." When we talk about "redemption" we are referring to the act of "buying"—particularly buying out of slavery. There's a transaction that takes place—a purchase out of slavery and into freedom. This redemption is why God the Son came in the flesh—to save his people by means of this transaction.

> 17 For God did not send his Son into the world to condemn the world, but in order that the world through him might be saved. (John 3:17)

In other words, the Son of God entered into his own creation to *redeem* his people. How did he do this?

The greatest redemption the world has ever known, required the greatest price ever paid—the blood of the very Son of God. And this blood was used to purchase a people who were and are enslaved to sin and death.

Now, the reason why Jesus' blood needed to be the currency for this redemption is because his life was the only life that was unblemished by sin. He was pure and spotless, living a perfectly obedient life—the life that Adam was supposed to live—the life that we all were supposed to live.

15 For we do not have a high priest who is unable to sympathize with our weaknesses, but one who in every respect has been tempted as we are, *yet without sin.* (Hebrews 4:15)

The perfect life of Jesus means everything for the Christian because it is the highest premium in the redemptive purchase. With Jesus' perfect life, and in his submission to the Father, his perfect death, there lies the Great Transaction—life for life and death for death.

3 For I delivered to you as of first importance what I also received: that Christ died for our sins in accordance with the Scriptures… (1 Corinthians 15:3)

Our statement says that Jesus "died a substitutionary death, having been crucified on a cross to atone for our sins." What does it mean that Jesus' death was "substitutionary"? Life for life, and death for death.

In Jesus' life and death, by our faith in him, his death not only forgave us of all of our sins and atoned for them all, but his life *brought* us life as well. By faith in Jesus, he takes our sin and punishment on the cross, and we get his obedience, his life, and his well-deserved inheritance with the Father. It is the best transaction in the world for sinners. He gets our sin and death. We get his righteousness and life.

20 I have been crucified with Christ. It is no longer I who live, but Christ who lives in me. And the life I now live in the flesh I live by faith in the Son of God, who loved me and gave himself for me. (Galatians 2:20)

This is the gospel—the good news of Jesus—that Jesus lived the life I should have lived and for my sake he died the death I should have died. It truly is "The Great Exchange."

21 For our sake he made him to be sin who knew no sin, so that in him we might become the righteousness of God. (2 Corinthians 5:21)

Rose Bodily From the Dead

But while Jesus' death was necessary, it was equally necessary that he not stay dead, which is why our statement continues, "…rose bodily from the dead…" Paul continues in 1 Corinthians 15 by saying in verse 4,

4…that he was buried, that he was raised on the third day in accordance with the Scriptures… (1 Corinthians 15:4)

Ascended into the Heavens

The other half of God's gospel is that Jesus not only died for our sins, but God raised him up from the dead, and he ascended into the heavens to take his place at the Father's right hand. Our statement continues, "and ascended into the heavens as witnessed by many…"

Luke, the gospel writer, pens his account of this event in Luke 24:51-53.

> 51 While he blessed them, he parted from them and was carried up into heaven. 52 And they worshiped him and returned to Jerusalem with great joy, 53 and were continually in the temple blessing God. (Luke 24:51-53)

As Witnessed by Many

The Son of God lives today. Jesus lives in 2019. And we believe this, not incredulously, but with the credibility of eyewitnesses.

This is one of the more unique things about Christianity among the world religions. It is a faith that is grounded in historical events and subjects itself to historical scrutiny. Unlike other religions— whether it be Joseph Smith, Muhammad, or the Bhagwan—Christianity affirms that Jesus worked miracles among many, died, and rose again and then appeared to many. In 1 Corinthians 15, Paul continues in verses 5-8.

> 5…and that he appeared to Cephas, then to the twelve. 6 Then he appeared to more than five hundred brothers at one time, most of whom are still alive, though some have fallen asleep. 7 Then he appeared to James, then to all the apostles. 8 Last of all, as to one untimely born, he appeared also to me. (1 Corinthians 15:5-8)

Many witnessed his death. Many witnessed his resurrection (at one time, a crowd of 500 witnessed Jesus after his crucifixion). Many witnessed his ascension. Jesus is not an idea, myth, or legend. His miraculous events are recorded in history. Christianity is a religion that subjects itself to this type of scrutiny because it places its claims within history. Therefore, we have the ability to confirm and affirm the trueness of Jesus' life, death, resurrection, and ascension.

At the Right Hand of the Father

Jesus' redemptive work was finished as he was nailed to that old wooden cross, where cried out, "It is finished." The purchase was complete and our redemption sure. But there was other work still to be had. Upon Jesus's ascension, he wasn't lifted up to the heavens so that he could take a nap. He didn't go on vacation. The Bible says that he ascended with the purpose of continuing his work to this very day.

> 1 My little children, I am writing these things to you so that you may not sin. But if anyone does sin, we have an advocate with the Father, Jesus Christ the righteous. (1 John 2:1)

Jesus continually advocates on our behalf in the fullness of God's presence. Both you and I need such an advocate before the Father—someone to plead our case—someone who is qualified to stand in the perfect and pure presence of God Almighty. This advocate is Jesus. He is presently the mediator between God and man. There is no need for popes, saints, or Mary to stand in our stead. We have one mediator with the Father, Jesus Christ the righteous.

This is why our statement says that Jesus "now advocates at the right hand of the Father on behalf of those who believe in Him." Jesus is standing between the Father and the believer saying, "Father, they are mine. I bought them with my blood. They are mine. And they are yours."

> 22…whether Paul or Apollos or Cephas or the world or life or death or the present or the future—*all are yours, and you are Christ's, and Christ is God's.* (1 Corinthians 3:22-23)

> 25 Consequently, he is able to save to the uttermost those who draw near to God through him, *since he always lives to make intercession for them.* (Hebrews 7:25)

Jesus is at the right hand of the Father, and it is there that we also reside. There is no price we could ever pay to get us into that holy presence except for the blood of Jesus. And it is ours only by faith in him.

Come and Rest in the Son of God

These truths are powerful—powerful enough to transform the rebels heart. Many who are still in rebellion against God may be uncertain about their eternal destiny, even if they may demonstrate indifference toward God on the outside. But in the quiet of the night, there lingers that uncertainty—one that we may even possess ourselves.

We may be unsure of how God looks upon us. It may be that in the end, we only hope that our good outweighs our bad. There are some—maybe even some reading this right now—who burrow themselves in their pillows at night under a load of guilt, hiding in the shadows of shame and tunneling in the terror of God's judgment.

Even as Christians, we sometimes seek to medicate our spiritual pain with revelry and play, or we scourge ourselves with suffering, all in the hopes to silence the cacophony of our consciences. We might try and read our Bibles more. We might resolve to pray longer. We might give more money to the church.

But this Pillar reminds us that there is rest for the weary soul by faith in Christ. There is peace preached to the heart filled with turmoil and conflict. Jesus only bids us, "Come!" and find that rest.

> 28 Come to me all you weary and heaven burdened and I will give you rest. 29 Take my yoke upon you and learn from me for I am lowly and gentle in heart and you will find rest for your souls. (Matthew 11:28-29)

Pillar 4 Endnotes

[1] Joe Rigney has a wonderful book on this called *The Things of Earth*. In the first chapter he argues, "...we can say that from all eternity God has had with him an image, a representation, a reflection of his own infinite perfection and beauty, and through this image has fully and completely known, understood, and expressed himself." Joe Rigney, *The Things of Earth: Treasuring God by Enjoying His Gifts* (Wheaton, Illinois: Crossway, 2015), p. 38.

[2] Some false beliefs about Jesus and his nature are Docetism (Cerinthus), adoptionism, and modalism. 1) Docetism affirms that Jesus was a spirit with the semblance of a man. An offshoot of Docetism was the belief taught by Cerinthus that God inhabited Jesus at his baptism and left him at the cross. 2) Adoptionism denies the eternal pre-existence of Jesus. 3) Modalism affirms that God has changed form—from the Father, to the Son, then to the Spirit. All of these have been rejected by the Church historically and deemed heresies.

[3] While this verse is taken from the ESV translation, they also provide a footnote at the bottom that indicates that this word "by" should be read "by means of", thus indicating that Jesus is not the "originator" but the "means" of creation. This is further confirmed in verse 16 where Paul clarifies what he means by saying, "all things were created through him, and for him."

Pillar 5
God the Holy Spirit

Affirmation

Regarding the nature of God the Holy Spirit, we believe that He is eternally proceeding from God the Father and God the Son, while comprehending and revealing the thoughts of God.

John 14:26; 15:26; 1 Corinthians 2:8-11

As to God the Holy Spirit's work, we believe He is sent by the Father and Son [1] to convict the world of sin, righteousness, and judgment [2], to bring to spiritual life from spiritual death [3], and to permanently indwell the saints [4], sealing [5], sanctifying [6], guiding [7], teaching [9], equipping [8], and comforting [10] all those who believe in Jesus.

[1] John 7:39, 14:26-27, 15:26; [2] John 16:8; [3] John 3:6-8;
[4] Romans 8:9; [5] Ephesians 1:13; [6] Ezekiel 36:26-27; [7] John 16:13;
[8] 1 Corinthians 12:7-10; [9] Ezekiel 36:26-27; [10] Acts 9:31

The Person of the Holy Spirit

Who is the Holy Spirit? The first word in this question is important. "Who?" Notice the question is not, "*What* is the Holy Spirit?" Our statement begins:

"Regarding the nature of God the Holy Spirit, we believe that He…"

The first thing we believe about God the Holy Spirit is that he is a "he". This may seem obvious to some, but to others it's not. When we hear the word "spirit", we can easily think of some sort of ethereal impersonal entity. It's all too often thought that a spiritual entity exists somewhere "out there" but not concerned with any of our affairs.

As a handyman, working among predominantly college students, I hear this type of worldview espoused all the time. The week that I was preaching on the Holy Spirit in this sermon series I was unclogging a young lady's kitchen sink while she stood there yamming about her life's woes—something to do with her roommate who had committed the unspeakable crime of leaving her unwashed dishes in the sink. But she got the last laugh. Those horrible things eventually came back to her roommate when she got slapped with some fines from the complex. And so she punctuated her laments with, "Karma got her good. The universe finally caught up to her…"

This type of belief is not uncommon, especially here in the Pacific Northwest. Most recognize some sort of spiritual realm, but often fail to attribute personhood in it. To them, the spirit realm— Karma—the universe—is just a non-personal force.

This is not the Divine Spirit that *The Bible* talks about. *The Bible* shows us that the Spirit of God is in fact a person.

> "26 But the Helper, the Holy Spirit, whom the Father will send in my name, he will teach you all things and bring to your remembrance all that I have said to you." (John 14:26)

The Holy Spirit's Personhood in Greek Grammar

I want to point something out in this passage regarding the personhood of the Holy Spirit using the original language.

Greek nouns, like Spanish or Latin, have gender, meaning that every noun can be classified as masculine, feminine, or neuter. And guess what gender "spirit" is? It's a neuter noun. This is important because Greek pronouns—nouns like *he*, *she*, or *it*—have to agree in gender with the noun they are referring to. English is the same way.

For example, if I say, "I'm sure *Taylor* can do 13 pull-ups today," as a follow up I could say, "*He* did 12 last week." I wouldn't use the pronoun "she" or "it" because the pronoun has to agree in gender. This is also the case with the Greek language.

However, while the Holy Spirit is a neuter noun in John 14:26, the pronoun John uses is masculine. "*He* will teach you." Grammatical consistency would normally dictate the author to say, "*It* will teach you." But John has other plans. He doesn't want to use "it" because the Holy Spirit is not an "it". The Holy Spirit is a "he". John will bend grammar rules to insist the personhood of the Holy Spirit.

This tells us, in John's mind, that the Holy Spirit is more than an entity. He has personhood. The Holy Spirit is not an "it" as the grammar should indicate. Rather the Holy Spirit is a "he"—the third person in the Trinity. *He* is a person, taking on the attributes of a person in loving, comforting, and grieving, just as a person does. So this is the first point of the affirmation. But we continue:

> "He is eternally proceeding from God the Father and God the Son..."

Eternally Proceeding

As was the case with God the Son, God the Holy Spirit also proceeds. The only difference is that the Holy Spirit proceeds from both the Father and the Son. Looking again at John 14:26, the Apostle writes,

> "26 But the Helper, the Holy Spirit, whom *the Father will send* in my name..."(John 14:26)

Then, a chapter later in John 15, the Apostle again records Jesus' words regarding the Holy Spirit.

> "26 But when the Helper comes, whom *I will send* to you from the Father, the Spirit of truth, *who proceeds from the Father*, he will bear witness about me." (John 15:26)

Equal with God

We must be careful here to avoid conflating the value of a person with the degree of their authority—especially in the Trinitarian community. Though the Holy Spirit proceeds from both the Father and Son, he also shares in the full divine essence of God. He is not less than the Father or Son, though he submits to both. He is equally God. Acts 5:3-4 demonstrates this very thing.

> 3 But Peter said, "Ananias, why has Satan filled your heart *to lie to the Holy Spirit* and to keep back for yourself part of the proceeds of the land? 4 While it remained unsold, did it not remain your own? And after it was sold, was it not at your disposal? Why is it that you have contrived this deed in your heart? You have not *lied to man but to God.*" (Acts 5:3-4)

Notice that Luke equates the Holy Spirit with God. Peter says in verse three that Ananias has lied to the Holy Spirit. He then follows that by saying that he in fact lied to God. Why would Luke say it this way? Luke wanted to show that the Holy Spirit shares in the divine essence and fullness of God, like the Father and Son.

Because the Holy Spirit shares his essence, it then follows that he knows the inner thoughts of God, which is why our statement reads, "while comprehending and revealing His thoughts."

Comprehending and Revealing

The Holy Spirit has two functions when it comes to the mind of God. Let's first identify them in 1 Corinthians 2:10-11.

10…these things God has *revealed* to us through the Spirit. For the Spirit searches everything, even the depths of God. 11 For who knows a person's thoughts except the spirit of that person, which is in him? So also no one *comprehends* the thoughts of God except the Spirit of God. (1 Corinthians 2:10-11)

We see in this text that God reveals things to us through the Spirit. But the revelation that we are given by the Spirit is first dependent on the Spirit searching the depths of God. After all, you can only reveal what you know. Without the Spirit's comprehensive knowledge of God, we cannot comprehend God at all. This is why we use the word "comprehending" in our affirmation.

The Holy Spirit dives into the complex mind of God and searches it through in through. No other person does this. This is unique only to him. But this is only half of it. Returning to John 15:26 we can see that something amazing happened when Jesus sent the Holy Spirit. When the Holy Spirit was given to us, we also gained access to all that the Holy Spirit has searched. He reveals his findings and we now know the mind of God—not exhaustively, but truly.

The Holy Spirit's Work

So, the Holy Spirit searches, comprehends, and reveals the mind of God. But how else is the Holy Spirit working? Our affirmation reads:

"As to God the Holy Spirit's work, we believe He is sent by the Father and Son to convict the world of sin, righteousness, and judgment…"

While the Father's role is that of originator in both creation and redemption, and the Son's role is the execution in both, we see that the Holy Spirit's role is unique when it comes to the Trinitarian fellowship. Jesus says,

> "7 Nevertheless, I tell you the truth: it is to your advantage that I go away, for if I do not go away, the Helper will not come to you. But if I go, I will send him to you. 8 And when he comes, he will convict the world concerning sin and righteousness and judgment:" (John 16:7-8)

Jesus first describes the Holy Spirit as "the Helper". This is why the Church has given him the Greek name *paraklete* (helper). He helps. And while it is that Jesus's work is centered around one historical event —his life, death, and resurrection—we see the Holy Spirit's work is a constant interaction. He is the continual Helper.

How does he help? Jesus says in this passage that the Holy Spirit's work is to "convict the world of *sin* and *righteousness* and *judgment.*"

Convicts of Sin

First, the Holy Spirit convicts the world.[1] Now let's just think about this word "convict." It seems to evoke the image of a courtroom, and rightfully so. It's a legal term that describes someone who is found guilty of a criminal offense. The civil courts exist to hold people accountable for their wrong actions by *convicting* them of their crimes. The Holy Spirit operates the same way, but on a universal scale. He is the person who confirms to God's image-bearers that they have transgressed God's universal laws—that they have done something wrong.

Without the Holy Spirit, we all would become sociopathic. We would see nothing wrong with the heinous nature of murder, theft, or adultery. We would likely stand in the courtroom saying, "What's the big deal?" So this is where the Holy Spirit works.

The Holy Spirit's active role in humanity is making all of us aware of our sins against God in a way that grates against our heart and mind. Psychology has deemed this the *conscience*. But we know that it is the Holy Spirit convicting us. In this we can see that the Holy Spirit plays an important role in God's redemptive plan. So, how?

Some would call God a bigot for telling us that we are in the moral wrong. "Who is he to tell me what I can and can't do?" But the conviction that the Holy Spirit gives is actually a good thing.

When the Holy Spirit convicts, he is initiating the beginning stages of salvation by announcing to our heart and mind that something is terribly wrong with us—and more than we think. Without him, we would be like a stage-four cancer patient with no doctor to tell us that we're dying. The Holy Spirit is the Physician who diagnoses our peril. While his conviction may hurt our ego, it actually is a means of his grace to ensure that we are aware of our plight.[2]

Convicts of Righteousness

"8 And when he comes, he will convict the world concerning sin and *righteousness* and judgment…" (John 16:8)

In Jesus' words, we not only see that the Holy Spirit convicts of sin, but also of righteousness. Now this is an interesting concept, isn't it? Who among us has ever said, "The Lord really convicted me of my righteousness this week?" But this is precisely what Jesus says the Spirit does.

This conviction of righteousness is the type that shows us not only where we are doing things wrong, but where we are doing them right. The Holy Spirit is a teacher, like Jesus. Jesus, in his earthly ministry, was always teaching his disciples about righteous living. But Jesus knew that his time on earth was limited. And so, to ensure that his new disciples would continue in the righteousness of God, he sent the Holy Spirit to convict the world of that righteousness. Jesus has sent us a guide. The Holy Spirit helps us not only by convicting our sin, but convicting of righteousness.

Convict Concerning Judgment

> "8 And when he comes, he will convict the world concerning sin and righteousness and *judgment*…" (John 16:8)

The word "judgment" is another term that evokes the image of a courtroom. The Holy Spirit's role in conviction is not only to reveal the depravity of our sin and the way of righteousness, but also to implant in the human heart an expectation that one day all the wrongs will be made right—that the scales will be balanced. We call this justice.

If we've ever opened up a history book, we'll quickly notice within ourselves an insatiable hunger for things to be put right, while reading of all the things that have gone terribly wrong. The reason for this is that humanity has been so out of whack since the fall. And so the Holy Spirit creates in us a longing for moral equity. Despite our distaste for the word "judgment" we all long for it in some way. We ache for a judgment that can bring order to all the chaos we witness in our family, friendships, community, city, country and world. This is the work of the Holy Spirit—to convict concerning judgment.

To Bring to Spiritual Life from Spiritual Death

But conviction of humanity is only one aspect of the Holy Spirit's work. In John 16:7-8, we also learn that with God's people the Holy Spirit goes a step further. He not only convicts of sin, righteousness and judgment, for them, but he actually saves them as well.

Our statement says, "to bring to spiritual life from spiritual death."[3] The Holy Spirit convicts, but he also saves. By his conviction he, in a sense, creates a problem in the conscience of all of humanity. But with God's redeemed people, he goes beyond the conviction and actually solves the problem.

The *Bible* shows us that in our sin, our hearts have died. And the only remedy for a dead heart is to resurrect it—to birth a new heart. This resurrection of the heart is the Spirit's work. Jesus says,

> "6 That which is born of the flesh is flesh, and that which is born of the Spirit is spirit. 7 Do not marvel that I said to you, 'You must be born again.' 8 The wind blows where it wishes, and you hear its sound, but you do not know where it comes from or where it goes. So it is with everyone *who is born of the Spirit.*" (John 3:6-8)

In order to have fellowship with God, the Holy Spirit must birth in us a new heart. If our heart is enslaved to sin, and we are in fact dead in our trespasses, and furthermore our flesh is hell-bent on warring against God, the only rescue from our hostility is to have our old heart ripped out, and replaced with a new one. It's a spiritual heart-transplant performed by the Great Surgeon.[4]

To Indwell the Saints

But his work doesn't stop here. It even goes further. For the people of God, the Holy Spirit not only convicts of sin and gives a new heart, but he also takes up permanent residence in them. God says,

"26 And I will give you a new heart, and a new spirit I will put within you. And I will remove the heart of stone from your flesh and give you a heart of flesh. 27 And I will put my Spirit within you, and cause you to walk in my statutes and be careful to obey my rules." (Ezekiel 36:26-27)

The Holy Spirit doesn't do a "touch and go" routine in our sanctification. He's not a special ops agent who drops in, gives us a new heart, and then says, "See ya!" No. When he drops in, he moves in. He takes up residence in the battlefield of our hearts and is resolved to stay in the trenches until the war is won. This is why our statement reads, "and to permanently indwell the saints." Paul says in Romans 8:9-11,

9 You, however, are not in the flesh but in the Spirit, if in fact the Spirit of God *dwells in you*. Anyone who does not have the Spirit of Christ does not belong to him. 10 But if Christ is in you, although the body is dead because of sin, the Spirit is life because of righteousness. 11 If the Spirit of him who raised Jesus from the dead *dwells in you*, he who raised Christ Jesus from the dead will also give life to your mortal bodies through his Spirit *who dwells in you*. (Romans 8:9-11)

Sealing and Sanctifying

Three times Paul affirms that the Spirit of God has chosen to take up permanent residence in his people. In his letter to the Ephesians he uses the word "seal".

13 In him you also, when you heard the word of truth, the gospel of your salvation, and believed in him, *were sealed with the promised Holy Spirit,* 14 who is the guarantee of our inheritance until we acquire possession of it, to the praise of his glory. (Ephesians 1:13-14)

The reason why Paul uses words like *promise*, *seal*, and *guarantee* is to assure us that he will never give up on us. There is no mess-of-a-heart too great for him to clean. The Holy Spirit has sealed us for the presence of God and has promised to continue his work in us until we obtain that inheritance. There's a word for this type of work—*sanctify*. To sanctify means to make holy, just as God is holy.

If we return to Ezekiel 36:27 we can see his sanctifying work when he says that he will *"cause* you to walk in my statutes." This verse doesn't mean that we then become robots, with no personhood, nor that God is controlling us in such a way. We are not lifeless puppets. But what it does mean is that our heart-orientation has changed from rebellion to obedience. We are no longer compelled to obey God against the will of our dead, sinful heart. We now *want* to obey. It's not that we won't ever sin. We just don't love sin anymore. Our desires have now aligned with God's desires.

Guiding and Teaching

Now, the *way* in which he persists in his sanctifying work is no mere magic trick, or flick of a switch. The Holy Spirit sanctifies by means of his continual instruction—his teaching, guiding, and equipping. Returning to John 16:13, Jesus promises,

"13 When the Spirit of truth comes, he will *guide* you into all the truth, for he will not speak on his own authority, but whatever he hears he will speak, and he will *declare* to you the things that are to come." (John 16:13)

Jesus tells us that the Spirit's work is to guide us into all truth and declare to us the things that are to come. This may very well be one of the passages that is only for the Apostles. However, we do also see in other portions of *Scripture* where the same principle applies. How? The way in which the Holy Spirit speaks is in his God-spirited—God-breathed holy word.

16 All Scripture is breathed out[5] by God and profitable for teaching, for reproof, for correction, and for training in righteousness… (2 Timothy 3:16)

God speaks, instructs, and declares to us through his Word His unchanging word—breathed out—is for our guidance and in this way, the Spirit instructs.

Equipping

Another part of the Holy Spirit's work is not only to instruct us for our own edification, but also for the edification of others. He teaches us how to minister to one another, just as he has ministered to us.

If we look at the Holy Spirit's work, we will notice that the means of his instructions involves his people. He equips us to equip one another, by his Spirit.

Now, this word "equip" is intentional. It implies warfare. And warfare, no doubt, is a major theme of the New Testament and the Christian life. We are to contend (Jude 3), wage war (1 Timothy 1:18), stand firm (Ephesians 6:13), persevere (Ephesians 6:18), and fight the good fight (2 Timothy 4:7). What should be evident in this type of vocabulary is that the Christian life is anything but passive, because God is anything but passive. The Christian life is a life of activity and warfare. And it's a life that that the Holy Spirit equips us for, *through* one another.

> 7 To each is given the manifestation of the Spirit for the common good. 8 For to one is given through the Spirit the utterance of wisdom, and to another the utterance of knowledge according to the same Spirit, 9 to another faith by the same Spirit, to another gifts of healing by the one Spirit, 10 to another the working of miracles, to another prophecy, to another the ability to distinguish between spirits, to another various kinds of tongues, to another the interpretation of tongues. (1 Corinthians 12:7-10)

The Holy Spirit works by means of his people working. We can see him at work in this passage when the gifts that he has given are exercised by his church and for his church—to equip them to faithfully engage in spiritual warfare in the Christian life.

Beware the Abuse of Gifts

A word of caution is warranted here simply because of the prevalence of certain misunderstandings concerning the Holy Spirit's work with regard to these gifts.

In some denominational circles, the emphasis of the Holy Spirit lies mainly on these gifts—specifically the gifts of tongues, healing, and prophecy. Most of us are familiar with TV preachers who espouse this type of teaching and pander to the masses with nonsensical emotionalism. To be "Spirit-filled" to them, means that you manifest supernatural oddities like being "drunk in the Spirit" or shaking uncontrollably—perhaps barking like a dog and clucking like a chicken.

But this is an incorrect view of both the Holy Spirit and his gifts. The gifts of the Spirit are given not to benefit the individual, but to serve the wider church for her common good.

As the body of Christ, we have not yet arrived at the completion of who we are in Jesus. Therefore, we need the Holy Spirit's gifts in order to sanctify us both personally and collectively.

All of the gifts mentioned in 1 Corinthians 12 are intended to be shared within the community and for the edification of the local church body. The Holy Spirit is equipping us individually to contribute to the whole, and is equipping the whole to minister to the individual.

These "manifestations" of the Spirit—like holy drunkenness or barking like a dog—do not contribute to the well-being and sanctification of the whole. They seem to reek of manipulation and self-aggrandizing, and therefore don't seem to be a genuine work of the Holy Spirit.

Comforting

So, we've seen so far, that the Holy Spirit teaches, guides, and equips. These are all necessary components of spiritual warfare. But what happens when we are wounded? The Holy Spirit not only prepares us for battle, but he is also there to nurture our wounds. He is our healer. Our affirmation says,

> "to permanently indwell the saints, therefore sealing, sanctifying, teaching, guiding, equipping, and *comforting...*"

What may be lost in the sanctifying process is the understanding that the process is often painful. In warfare, there is always a cost. Peter compares the people of God to gold being put in fire for purification. (1 Peter 1:7) With Peter, the point is that sanctification burns, but burns for our benefit.

When we walk through flames, we not only need armor and the strength of a soldier (Ephesians 6:13), but also the soothing affection of a loving God—the nurturing of a wounded soul. This is also the arena of the Holy Spirit.

> 31 So the church throughout all Judea and Galilee and Samaria had peace and was being built up. And walking in the fear of the Lord and in the *comfort* of the Holy Spirit, it multiplied. (Acts 9:31)

God embraces us in our pain. We not only *know* his grace and comfort in his word, but we experience it on a personal level. We know his peace in our hearts.

Paul, in his opening salutations, often personifies the Holy Spirit as this experiential grace and peace.

> 2 *Grace* to you and *peace* from God our Father and the Lord Jesus Christ. (2 Corinthians 1:2)

Of course God the Father and Son are apparent in this passage. But if God is triune, where is the Holy Spirit? To answer this, let's look at John 14:26-27. Jesus says,

> "26 But the Helper, the *Holy Spirit*, whom the Father will send in my name, he will teach you all things and bring to your remembrance all that I have said to you. 27 *Peace* I leave with you; my *peace* I give to you." (John 14:26-27)

"So where is the Holy Spirit?" At first glance, it may not seem apparent, but if we turn a few pages over to John 20:21-22, we can start to put some of these pieces together that show how comfort, peace, and the Holy Spirit are all related.

> "21 Jesus said to them again, "*Peace* be with you. As the Father has sent me, even so I am sending you." 22 And when he had said this, he *breathed* on them and said to them, "Receive the *Holy Spirit*. (John 20:21-22)

Now, why are we bringing these two scriptures together? What do they have common? If we place them side-by-side, we will notice that they both tell us something about the Holy Spirit—something about his nature—that his nature *is* peace.

Jesus is described as sending the Holy Spirit, and immediately after he says, "*Peace* I leave with you; my *peace* I give to you." He then breathes on them and says, "Receive the Holy Spirit." What can we conclude? *The Holy Spirit is the peace of God.*

If we understand the Holy Spirit to be the embodiment of God's peace, then we can see that he is also present in Paul's salutations. The Holy Spirit is the *grace* and *peace* that come from the Father and the Lord Jesus Christ.

Grace and Peace Extended

All of this becomes important for our own sanctification, especially while we are afflicted this side of eternity. It's important because that same affection—that grace and peace that the Holy Spirit possesses is also accessible to us. Paul writes in 2 Corinthians 1:3-4,

> 3 Blessed be the God and Father of our Lord Jesus Christ, the Father of *mercies* and God of all *comfort*, 4 who *comforts* us in all our affliction, so that we may be able to *comfort* those who are in any affliction, with the *comfort* with which we ourselves are *comforted* by God. (2 Corinthians 1:3-4)

Our God is the God of all comfort who comforts us in our afflictions. And while he comforts us, he is also teaching us what it means to comfort. He teaches us to be like him—to comfort like he comforts. He is the necessary comfort for the saints, full of *grace* and *peace* and indwelling all those who are afflicted.

All Those Who Believe in the Son

Finally, our statement concludes with "...to those who believe in Jesus." All that we could ever want in fellowship with the eternal God—a newly-birthed heart, a purified and holy life, the assistance of God in guiding, teaching, and equipping us for every good work, and his eternal comfort—all of that is accessible by faith in Jesus. While our hearts long for the grace and peace from God our Father and the Lord Jesus Christ, most never find it. But it's promised to those who trust in Christ alone.

Blessedly Assured

The Holy Spirit has given us a blessed assurance. He has guaranteed that by the blood of Jesus that we are his. The Holy Spirit has sealed us and therefore we have assurance that nothing can separate us from the love of God. Hear now these precious promises.

"I am yours and you are mine!" (Song of Solomon 6:3)

"I will be your God, and you shall be my people!" (Jeremiah 7:23)

"...you were sealed for the day of redemption." (Ephesians 4:30)

"He who began a good work in you will bring it to completion at the day of Jesus Christ." (Philippians 1:6)

Pillar 5 Endnotes

[1] When John uses the word "world", he most likely means "humanity". The Apostle loves to use this word with a variety of nuances.

[2] During the Question and Answer time at our church one individual asked about certain people whom it seemed did not possess these convictions. We refer to them as sociopaths. This is a multi-layered question, but in short, there are a couple explanations for such people. 1) Their sinful patterns have developed over time by the continual searing of the conscience. Typically, we find ourselves to think of evil more acceptable if we commit evil in gradual stages. If someone lies for the first time, the lie is likely to prick the conscience in a way that is noticeably uncomfortable. However, when one finds oneself lying on a regular basis, the lies become more normal and therefore acceptable. There develops callouses on the soul, so to speak, like the hands of seasoned mason-worker who no longer feels the sting of the shovel gripped in his hands. 2) A second explanation is that some are born with this disposition. We live in a fallen world. Paul reminds us in Romans 8 that at the fall of Adam, "the world was subjected to futility", which means that everything is broken—creation, internal organs, sexuality, and yes even our mental state. The reason for some being born with little capacities for moral conviction is that something is profoundly wrong within their make-up.

[3] It's important to note that when we say "spiritual death" and "spiritual life" that we are not speaking in a figurative sense. This is reality. In sin, the soul of a man is dead —*literally* dead. Although this death isn't physical, nevertheless it's real.

[4] The "heart transplant" is often referred to in theological terms as "regeneration" or being "born again".

[5] The term here "God-breathed" is actually a compound word that Paul quite possibly made-up. We explored this briefly in the first pillar. It contains *theos*, meaning God, and *pneuo*—the same word for "spirit" or "breath".

Pillar 6
Humanity and Its Destiny

Affirmation

Regarding humanity, we believe that we were created in the image of God [1], first with Adam from the dust of the ground, and then Eve from Adam's side [2]. Thus, they are the historical parents of the human race, originally being without sin, and created to love and enjoy God.[3]

[1] Genesis 1:26-27; [2] Genesis 2:7; [3] Genesis 1:22, 28

We believe that although God created mankind upright [1], our first parents were led into sin by personal disobedience to the revealed will of God [2]. It was in this manner they fell from their original innocence and communion with God. [3].

[1] Ecclesiastes 7:29a; [2] Ecclesiastes 7:29b; Romans 1:21-23; Genesis 3:17; [3] Genesis 3:1-7

Thereby, as head of the human race, through Adam's fall became the fall of all his posterity, thus separating humanity from God, and properly incurring a nature of corruption, hostility, guilt, death, and condemnation.

Romans 1:21-32; 3:23; 5:9-10, 12-19; 1 Corinthians 15:21-22; Colossians 2:13

Therefore, we believe that every human being is enslaved to sin [1], and morally incapable [2] of loving and honoring God, and therefore facing eternal judgment and wrath from Him [3].

[1] John 8:34; [2] Romans 6:16, 20, 23; 8:7-8; [3] John 3:36

Humanity

So far, we've primarily focused on the nature and work of God as revealed in *Scripture*. But now, we'll take a hard shift and turn our attention toward humanity—the image-bearers of God. In this pillar, we'll explore mankind's original nature, and our corruption that soon followed in the creation account. To do this, we must go to the beginning—to the first book of *The Bible*—Genesis. Genesis gives us the clearest account of our origin, why we were made, and what's wrong with us.

Created in the Image of God

Our statement begins by affirming that humans were created in the image of God. Genesis 1 uses these exact words.

> 26 Then God said, "Let us make man in our image, after our likeness. And let them have dominion over the fish of the sea and over the birds of the heavens and over the livestock and over all the earth and over every creeping thing that creeps on the earth."
>
> 27 So God created man *in his own image*,
> *in the image of God* he created him;
> male and female he created them.
> (Genesis 1:26-27)

So what does it mean to be created "in the image of God?" Does it mean that we take on the physical characteristics of God? Does it mean that God has two eyes, arms and legs, and a belly button? No. Not only does the text mention nothing about physical appearance, but

The Bible also tells us that God is spirit in John 4:24, as we've already seen.

So if it's not physical, then what is this particular image that we bear? Notice the context of Genesis 1. God gives a commission to the man and woman to "have dominion" over all creation, which immediately follows the statement that we are made in God's image. This means that one of the ways that human beings bear God's image is that they not only possess the *capacity* to exercise dominion, using their intellect, morality, and ingenuity, but it also means that they are given the *responsibility* to do so. In other words, humanity, in bearing the image of God, possesses a dignity, worth, complexity, and responsibility unlike any other created thing. We, as humans, bear his image alone in this way and therefore we possess uniqueness within the eyes of God.

Adam from Dust and Eve From Adam's Side

Our affirmation continues with the specifics of mankind's creation. *How* were both male and female created?

"...first with Adam from the dust of the ground, and then Eve from Adam's side..."

We can see in Genesis 2:7 and 2:21-22 the uniqueness of Adam and Eve's creation. Let's first look at how Adam was created.

7 Then the LORD God formed the man of dust from the ground and breathed into his nostrils the breath of life, and the man became a living creature... (Genesis 2:7)

We witness here the power of the Life-Giver, breathing his own life into something that possessed none. He takes that which is inanimate, and animates it.

Now the way in which God created man is different than the way he created woman. He takes his own breath—his spirit—and breathes into the dust to give him a soul.[1] Mankind, without the breath of God, is nothing more than a pile of dust. There is a certain humility that comes along with that. But also, it is with the breath of God that man stands distinguished among the rest of God's creation. There is a certain dignity that comes along with that. And this is how Adam was created. Now, what about the woman?

With regard to the woman, we find her creation account later in Genesis 2:21-22.

> 21 So the LORD God caused a deep sleep to fall upon the man, and while he slept took one of his ribs and closed up its place with flesh. 22 And the rib that the LORD God had taken from the man he made into a woman and brought her to the man. (Genesis 2:21-22)

This account is unique altogether. Upon seeing that there was no suitable helper among all of God's creatures for the man, God took from the man's side—his very flesh and bone—to make for him a helper. God then brings her back to the man.[2]

A couple things are worth noting regarding the woman's account. First, notice that the woman was created not behind the man as an inferior—nor was she created from the front of the man as a superior. Rather, she was created from his side, as a helper. Matthew Henry so beautifully wrote in his commentary that the woman was made, "near to his heart to be loved by him."[3] She was made from his side.

Secondly, we can see God's *modus operandi* in his redemptive plan in the woman's creation account. He takes out of the man, creates the woman, and then brings her back to the man. In other words, God rips apart only to mend and make better than it was before. Is this not how God accomplishes his redemptive work as well? We see this especially in the life and death of Jesus. Jesus' body was ripped apart and made whole, so that we who were far away from God, like Eve, might be brought back to him.

So, the differences between the male and female creation accounts are profound and demonstrate the unique value that God has given us. The man was made from dust, with the breath of God. The woman was made from the man. And both were made in the image of God. And although both were created differently, (note that both were not created *ex nihilo*), both reflect the image of God.

> 27 So God created man in his own image,
> in the image of God he created him;
> male and female he created them.
> (Genesis 1:27)

Historical Parents

"Thus, they are the historical parents of the human race…" Our affirmation continues with "historical parents" because a great effort has been made in the past couple hundred years to remove God

135

out of the origin of his world. It's commonly held, and in many cases assumed, that the world was not spoken into existence, but rather our world is a product of random chaos slowly coming into order—human beings included. In this view, we are not a product of intent, but of time and chance acting on matter—that we *evolved* from simple cells, to more complex cell-clusters, to living organisms, to primates, and then to human beings.

Because we believe *The Bible* as God's word, we therefore affirm that Adam and Eve were "the historical parents of the human race..."

Created Without Sin to Glorify God

Now, as image-bearers of a holy God, Adam and Eve also reflected God's moral perfection. They were untainted from sin. This doesn't mean, however, that they were complete or mature in their spiritual development. Rather, both possessed no moral blemishes, like a strong, healthy apple tree that has yet to produce big, red apples.

It's in this way that Adam and Eve were created "without sin" in the paradise garden. And they were created so that they would love God and enjoy him in all his manifold perfection, thus glorifying him.

So What Happened?

But it's no surprise that when we look out on the present world we can see how far we actually are from said paradise. When we watch the news, we see anything but loving, enjoying, and glorifying God.[4] So what happened? How did we get here? Will we ever return? Genesis helps us with these questions by first telling us what became of our historical parents and the consequences of their actions that followed thereafter.

Led Into Sin

Our affirmation states that both Adam and Eve were "led into sin by personal disobedience." It's *personal* because each individual was accountable to God. Adam didn't incur judgment for Eve's disobedience, nor Eve for Adam's. So how did this personal disobedience unfold?

As we open up Genesis 3 we are immediately introduced to a serpent. And the serpent is approaching the woman to deceive her. He begins his deception by mainly doing two things: 1) Perverting the *Word of God* and 2) undermining God's goodness and love for them.

Regarding the first point of deception, we see that the serpent's initial words to the woman are, "Did God actually say, 'You shall not eat of any tree in the garden?'" (Genesis 3:1). We should be quick to note that this is not what God said to Adam. God commanded Adam first, "You shall surely eat of every tree of the garden." (Genesis 2:16, My translation)[5] The initial command was to enjoy every tree—every tree but one. But the serpent twisted God's words to make it seem that God was withholding something good from them, thus undermining the goodness of God. The shrewd question, "Did God really say…" was enough to embed a seed of doubt in Eve. She questioned whether God loved them and cared for them, and had their best in mind. Seeing this, the serpent doubled down on her doubt by then placing God and mankind in opposition to one another. Look at verse 5.

> "5 For God knows that when you eat of it your eyes will be opened, and you will be like God, knowing good and evil." (Genesis 3:5)

The serpent now appeals to Eve's independence, freedom, and self-governance. And so the woman, now believing the snake, takes the fruit from the one tree that they were prohibited to eat from, and she eats…and oh, by the way, Adam is right there following her lead in quiet submission.

Both Adam and Eve disobeyed God. In a whole garden of "Eat!" they had a single, "Don't eat!" And because they probably had the most severe case of FOMO (fear of missing out), they both ignored the revealed will of God and sinned by deciding to do things their own way. This is why our statement says, "It was in this manner they fell from their original innocence and communion with God."

Fall from Innocence

In both Adam and Eve's disobedience, sin entered the world and they broke communion with God. They were no longer innocent. This is most apparent in their immediate reaction following their disobedience. They hid because they were full of shame. Verse 7 says:

> 7 the eyes of both were opened, and they knew they were naked, and they sewed fig leaves together and made themselves loincloths. (Genesis 3:7)

Adam could no longer trust Eve with the intimacy of his body, nor could Eve with Adam. They were both susceptible to harm because of sin and were full of shame. Innocence was lost. Communion with God was broken. Life now had a beginning and an end. And both were banished from paradise.

23 therefore the LORD God sent him out from the garden of Eden to work the ground from which he was taken. 24 He drove out the man, and at the east of the garden of Eden he placed the cherubim and a flaming sword that turned every way to guard the way to the tree of life. (Genesis 3:23-24)

In trying to obtain the one thing that God said no to, they lost everything he said yes to. Sin was dwelling in them now. And as they carried out their commission to "be fruitful and multiply", sin would also be embedded in the fruit of Eve's womb, thus all their posterity would inherit it.

12 Therefore, just as sin came into the world through one man, and death through sin, and so death spread to all men because all sinned…(Romans 5:12)

The children of Adam   you and I—would receive through him, the inheritance of his disobedience—corruption, hostility, condemnation, and death.

Corruption
19 For as by the one man's disobedience the many were made sinners… (Romans 5:19)

Hostility
7 For the mind that is set on the flesh is hostile to God, for it does not submit to God's law; indeed, it cannot. (Romans 8:7)

Condemnation

12 …in order that all may be condemned who did not believe the truth but had pleasure in unrighteousness.
(2 Thessalonians 2:12)

Death

21 For as by a man came death, by a man has come also the resurrection of the dead. 22 For as in Adam all die, so also in Christ shall all be made alive. (1 Corinthians 15:21-22)

Enslaved to Sin

Because everyone comes from Adam, and in Adam we all "were made sinners," our affirmation states "every human being is enslaved to sin."

34 Jesus answered them, "Truly, truly, I say to you, everyone who practices sin is a slave to sin. (John 8:34)

So what exactly does it mean to be a slave to sin? Furthermore, why specifically do we include this language in our affirmation?

Both Jesus and Paul are intentional in their use of slavery imagery. The Jews knew something of slavery in their own history. They knew the cruelty of Egypt and Babylon, and the destruction they caused their people. They knew firsthand, the realities of a slave and master relationship. They knew that their well-being was entirely in the hands of their master. A slave could only do what his master said. This had been proven to be true in their own heritage.

So Jesus and Paul both riff on slavery and essentially say,

"There's a new Pharaoh and a new Nebuchadnezzar, only this master is much more severe, and far more deadly. It's sin and you are its slave."

Now, let's connect the dots. If humans are slaves to sin, then we humans can do nothing but obey our sinful nature—a joyless and fruitless labor. Paul draws this out in Romans 6:16.

> 16 Do you not know that if you present yourselves to anyone as obedient slaves, you are slaves of the one whom you obey, either of sin, which leads to death, or of obedience, which leads to righteousness? (Romans 6:16)

It's because of this slavery that the human being is "morally incapable of loving and honoring God." We are born into this slavery and in dire need of deliverance.

> 7 For the mind that is set on the flesh is hostile to God, for it does not submit to God's law; indeed, it cannot. 8 Those who are in the flesh cannot please God. (Romans 8:7-8)

Incurring Judgment and Wrath

This hostility toward God warrants a judgment and wrath that is equal to the severity of the crime. He is the eternally holy God and an offense against him is deserving of the severest of punishments. Therefore, the wrath of the eternal God is the sentence, and death is the outcome.

23 For the wages of sin is death… (Romans 6:23)

Now, there are a couple ways to think of God's wrath. Typically, when we hear "the wrath of God" we think of a future event where God will finally pour out his anger on all who do evil. But the Apostle John also says that there is an active wrath of God that is presently exercised on all those who are enslaved to sin. He writes in John 3:36:

> 36 Whoever believes in the Son has eternal life; whoever does not obey the Son shall not see life, but *the wrath of God remains on him.* (John 3:36)

The Hope to Come

This portion of our statement is a sobering one. It's the part of the affirmation that if left alone would destroy us and leave us in despair. It certainly is a harsh reality that we are not inherently good before God. It is tough to accept that we have inherited the shame of our historical parents and are not inclined to comply with God's demands. It's sobering that we are naturally rebellious and therefore naturally deserving of God's wrath. As the Apostle Paul says, we "were by nature children of wrath." (Ephesians 2:3)

But the good news is that our statement doesn't end here, because *The Bible* doesn't end here. Yes, *The Bible* does inform us of our destiny apart from God, but *The Bible* also gives us a glorious hope in the deliverance from the slavery of sin and death into freedom and life found in a better garden, with a better Adam. Returning to Romans 5, Paul says:

19 For as by the one man's disobedience the many were made sinners, *so by the one man's obedience the many will be made righteous.* (Romans 5:19)

God would send another man—the second Adam—to solve the problem that the first Adam created in paradise. He would mend what sin had torn apart. Where Adam disobeyed and ushered in sin and death, Jesus—the perfect Son of God—would obey and usher in righteousness and life. This is the good news of Jesus Christ—that the people of God would not remain enslaved to sin, but by faith in him, he would set them free.

"35 The slave does not remain in the house forever; the son remains forever. 36 So if the Son sets you free, you will be free indeed." (John 8:35-36)

Pillar 6 Endnotes

[1] The Hebrew word נְשָׁמָה can mean both "breath" and "spirit".

[2] Some would say that this is the first marriage where the Father walks his daughter down the aisle to meet her husband. I like this comparison and think it's especially appropriate, given Paul's exposition on marriage in Ephesians 5:22-33 using the creation account.

[3] Matthew Henry, *Matthew Henry's Commentary* on the whole Bible.

[4] One of the evidences of this paradise is humanity's desire to return to it. This is most evident in many of the stories that are told throughout history. Most fiction contains themes of returning to paradise—to a state of happiness and wholeness—a longing engrained in the human heart.

[5] For those interested in the Hebrew, the verb תֹּאכֵל in Genesis 2:16 is a *qal* imperfect verb in the second person. This means that it can be translated using "may" or to emphasize the command more, "you shall," which is my rendering.

Pillar 7
Humanity and Salvation

Affirmation

We believe that God the Father, in His desire to save humanity, sent His Son—Jesus—to die as a sinless [1] substitute for sinners [2] once for all[3], and to rise from the dead, thus guaranteeing and securing the resurrection to eternal life for those who believe in Him [4] and His substitutionary work—which is the gospel.

[1] 2 Corinthians 5:21; [2] Romans 5:8-21, Titus 3:3-7; [3] Romans 6:10;
[4] 1 Corinthians 15:20-22, Philippians 3:20-21,
Colossians 1:21, 22, 2:13

We believe that because of man's corrupt nature and incapability to submit to God, God freely saves by regenerating the heart, by power of the Holy Spirit [1], through the hearing of the gospel—Jesus's life, death, resurrection and ascension [2]. It is His work that guarantees [3] redemption [4] for those who place their individual faith[5] in His person and work alone[6].

[1] Ezekiel 36:26-27; [2] 1 Corinthians 2:14, 15:3-5, 45
[3] Ephesians 1:14, Jude 24-25; [4] Hebrews 9:12; [5] Acts 17:30,
John 5:24, Romans 3:23-26; [6] Ephesians 2:8-9

God the Father and His Desire To Save

We begin with the Father's desire. Our affirmation reads: "We believe that God the Father, *in his desire* to save…" Let's pause and reflect on the word *desire*. We know desire to be the thing that drives us to action. And we all possess it. Whether the object of our desire is good or not, regardless, desire in itself is as sure as the air we breathe.

Now, as those who are created in the image of God, in addition to being creatures of desire, it should come as no shock that the Creator also has desire. We not only see his desire displayed in *Scripture*, but we see his desire displayed even in our desiring—as those who are made in his image. But that's as far as the similarities run when it comes to comparing our desire with God's desire.

There is a vast difference between the object of God's desire and man's desire. In fact, that which we desire often proves to be contrary to what God desires. And one of those desires, which is completely different from God's desire, is mercy. Where we are quick to execute revenge when wronged—God is quick to mercy.

> "23 Have I any pleasure in the death of the wicked, declares the Lord GOD, and not rather that he should turn from his way and live?" (Ezekiel 18:23)

The Father is foremost resolved to show mercy. In Ezekiel, it's plain that God's first desire is that the sinner would turn away from his sin and toward himself—away from death and toward life. God's primary desire is salvation and the preservation of our life, though we have wronged him.

We also see that God desire to save. The Apostle Paul reminds his spiritual son, Timothy, in his first letter that:

> 3 This is good, and it is pleasing in the sight of God our Savior, 4 who *desires* all people to be saved and to come to the knowledge of the truth. (1 Timothy 2:3-4)

This is why we begin with God's desire, and in particular, his desire to save. Salvation comes from the depths of the heart of God. Our God is a God who takes pleasure in saving, in offering mercy, in exercising compassion, and in extending forgiveness. How many of us could say this is our primary delight when sinned against? But lest we think that God's mercy, forgiveness and love come easy, we will now examine the cost of it all.

Sent His Son

Our affirmation says that God initiated his salvation plan by first sending his Son. John 3:16 is a resounding timeless truth concerning God's Son that still possesses tremendous power today.

> 16 For God, in this manner, loved the world, that he gave his only begotten Son. (John 3:16 *My translation*)

In John 3:16, we can see both the extent and the depth of God's saving desire. What did it cost the Father? It cost him his own Son.

When Jesus tells the parable of the man who inadvertently stumbled upon a treasure in a field in Matthew 13:44, he then describes the man's reaction. What was this man so compelled to do?

> "44 Then in his joy he goes and sells all that he has and buys that field." (Matthew 13:44)

This man was so joyfully compelled by his intense desire for the treasure in the field, that he took all of his possessions and sold them in order to obtain what his heart desired most. That was the cost—everything. This should make us wonder: What was the cost of God's desire to save us? And what could he possibly gain from it?

From eternity past, the Father looked at the Son—whom he had been in perfect unity and community with, and essentially said, "I need you to leave and go to them. I need you to live like they live—to die like they die, and depart from me so that we can have them together."

Now, God didn't send Adam. Nor did he send an angel or some other creature to save his people. No. God sent his own Son. God the Son would become a man and enter the world he made, not to execute justice on his rebellious creatures, though it would have been perfectly right for him to do so. He sent his own Son to save his rebellious creatures—to leave behind his divine prerogatives and "give his life as a ransom for many." (Mark 10:45)

That's what salvation cost him—an uncommon currency—a particular payment of incomparability—the perfect and pure blood of God's own Son—Jesus Christ.

But why was blood required, and furthermore, the blood of God's Son? Why couldn't our salvation be paid with money or treasure, as slave masters have always required? Why is it that "without the shedding of blood there is no forgiveness of sin," as Hebrews 9:22 says. In short, this is no ordinary slave-master, nor an ordinary redemption.

To Die as a Sinless Substitute for Sinners

As we've already seen, every human has been born into this world as a child "of wrath." (Ephesians 2:3) Naturally, we all stand before God, indicted on the charges of heavenly treason.

> 10 None is righteous, no not one. No one understands. No one seeks for God. (Romans 3:10)

Sin has broken fellowship and friendship with God. Sin has kept us from his perfect and pure presence. Sin is so atrocious and depraved, that it demands complete separation from him. It's an infinite offense that's deserving of an infinite punishment with a bail set at an infinite cost. No amount of money or rare possession could ever buy off the Judge. The cosmic crime required the highest premium—life for a life.

So God, instead of justly condemning his creatures, condemned our sin by condemning his sinless Son in our place. Jesus, the perfect and pure Son of God, died as sinless substitute in our place and demolished the barrier of sin that endured between us.

> 21 For our sake he made him to be sin who knew no sin, so that in him we might become the righteousness of God. (2 Corinthians 5:21)

> 21 but God shows his love for us in that while we were still *sinners, Christ died for us.* (Romans 5:8)

Once For All

Our statement continues with "...to die as a sinless substitute for sinners *once for all*..." What does this phrase "once for all" mean? The death of Christ was a one-time transaction. The blood of Jesus, spilled on that cross, was sufficient to pay for all the sins of all the people in all times. Now, this "one-time" sacrifice was an unusual concept for the first century Jews.

In the Old Testament sacrificial system, the Torah required sacrifice on a *daily* basis. The priests would regularly slaughter animals as a means of purification of sin. The author of Hebrews, knowing this, in light of Christ, says,

> 10 And by that will we have been sanctified through the offering of the body of Jesus Christ *once for all*. (Hebrews 10:10)

We see two implications from Hebrews 10:10. 1) The blood of animals could never take away sin. They weren't enough, even if offered on a daily basis. 2) The blood of Jesus, offered once, was sufficient to cleanse every sin ever committed against God. Jesus' life was that precious. His blood was that pure.

> 10 For the death he died he died to sin, once for all, but the life he lives he lives to God. (Romans 6:10)

To Rise Again

But the good message about Jesus doesn't end with his death, nor does our affirmation. Our affirmation then says, "…and to rise from the dead, thus guaranteeing and securing the resurrection to eternal life for those who believe in Him…"

While we know that we are saved, we should also have an understanding of what we are saved from. Yes, we have been bought out of the bondage of sin. But why even was sin so dangerous? What was sin producing in us that necessitated a particular deliverance? In other words, what was so wrong with our slave-master—sin? Paul tells us in 1 Corinthians 15:17-22 where the road of sin leads.

17 And if Christ has not been raised, your faith is futile and you are still in your sins. 18 Then those also who have fallen asleep in Christ have perished. 19 If in Christ we have hope in this life only, we are of all people most to be pitied. 20 *But in fact Christ has been raised from the dead*, the firstfruits of those who have fallen asleep. 21 For as by a man came *death*, by a man has come also *the resurrection of the dead*. 22 For as in Adam all *die*, so also in Christ shall all be made *alive*. (1 Corinthians 15:17-22)

Death is the product of sin. Sin produced death in us. That's a harsh slave-master—one who works you into the ground, six-feet under.

Yet *Christ died and delivered us from death*. Let's not miss the profound truth contained in this statement, just because we've heard it a number of times. Sometimes phrases like, "Christ died for my sins," can seem like a broad stroke of the spiritual brush, while we miss all the color on the canvas.

This deliverance from death means that we are brought into life. And the life that we are saved *into* is not just a spiritual life—which is very real. Neither has he saved into some sort of spiritually ethereal heaven out there—as heaven is often thought to be. No. God has saved us *into* the resurrection of our bodies. Our salvation is from death and into the spiritual world *and* the physical world.

This passage in Corinthians tells us that when we were saved by faith in Christ, not only were we delivered from the power of sin, but our spirit came alive and we were guaranteed a resurrection of our own bodies just as Jesus was resurrected in his body.

What does this mean for us? The implications of this truth are tremendous. When we believe that nothing can separate us from the love of God in Christ, *not even death*, then fear tends to tuck-tail and run. We are empowered to believe with a hardy assurance that nothing is able to separate us from God. Even death will not have the final say on our life. God will.

So when it comes time for us to die, we should be able to look our loved ones in the eyes with utmost sincerity and plead with them, "Please don't pay much for my coffin. I'm not staying there long. Christ will call me home very soon."

> 20 But we await a savior, the Lord Jesus Christ, who will transform our lowly bodies to be like his glorious one. (Philippians 3:20)

So Jesus' blood not only saves us from the bondage of sin and death, but it also saves us *into* life—both spiritual and physical—a soul and body incorruptible, immortal, and eternal. Oh, what a glorious gospel we have.

The Holy Spirit Regenerates the Heart

Our statement continues, "We believe that because of man's corrupt nature and incapability to submit to God, God freely saves by regenerating the heart, by power of the Holy Spirit…"

So far, we have explored the means by which God saves us—the blood of Jesus—in addition to what God saves us from—death—and what God saves us into—life. But now we turn our attention to the process. What happens *in us* and *to us* when God saves us?

As we've already seen, sin is the problem in our heart. The Bible tells us that we are inclined to exchange the glory of God for images. We forge gods in our own hearts and minds and are blinded to the truth and beauty of God.

> 7 For the mind that is set on the flesh is hostile to God, for it does not submit to God's law; indeed, it cannot. (Romans 8:7)

But our hearts don't act alone in this treachery against God. There is a co-conspirator in our *coup*.

> 4 In their case *the god of this world* has blinded the minds of the *unbelievers*, to keep them from seeing the light of the gospel of the glory of Christ, who is the image of God.
> (2 Corinthians 4:4)

The reason why we are incapable of submitting to God is because we are blind. We can't come to that which we can't see, and our lack of sight is attributed to two things in this passage—*unbelief* and *the god of this world*. We are unable to see the beauty and wonder of the eternal God. Paul describes this blindness as unbelief. But it doesn't act independently. Our minds conspire with *"the god of this world"*. The Devil jumps on our unbelief to blind us from seeing Jesus.

We all probably know people—or perhaps we are this person— who have sat in a church pew their whole life and have heard *The Bible* taught, have attended youth camps, yet still cannot submit to God or see Jesus as the treasure that he is. With this person, he is blind, though he possesses a *"Christian"* heritage.

Yet we who believe have tasted and seen that the Lord is good. (Psalm 34:8) We have experienced that moment when the light in our soul was flipped on. One moment we didn't believe and the next moment we did. One moment we were reading the words on the pages of *The Bible*, feeling nothing, and the next moment those same words were inescapable, captivating us with the wonder of God. That's called *faith*.

We believed. And why did we believe? Why did we believe in Christ that one particular time, but not the thousand other times before it? Was it because we finally wised up and made the right decision? No. As one musician said, "The blind won't gain their sight by opening their eyes."[1] That belief was the work of the Holy Spirit alone.

The theological word for this process is "regeneration." Regeneration is the Holy Spirit breathing new life into our dead heart and resurrecting our soul anew. The Lord promises through Ezekiel,

> "26 And *I will give you a new heart*, and *a new spirit I will put within you*. And I will remove the heart of stone from your flesh and give you a heart of flesh." (Ezekiel 36:26)

The Holy Spirit alone is the one who awakens the heart and lifts the blinders off our eyes and enables us to see the glory and beauty of Christ. Jesus describes this regeneration as being "born again."

"7 Do not marvel that I said to you, 'You must be born again.' 8 The wind blows where it wishes, and you hear its sound, but you do not know where it comes from or where it goes. So it is with everyone who is born of the Spirit." (John 3:7-8)

Through Hearing the Gospel

This is what happens when we first come to saving faith in Christ. But we should also note that the Holy Spirit doesn't act independently. Yes, he is sufficient to save, but he has also chosen that the means by which he saves is "…through the hearing of the gospel of Christ's life, death, and resurrection."

This is why there is a "gospel"—a good message. In the proclamation of this message, the Holy Spirit opens our heart to receive God in Jesus. When the Word of God meets the Holy Spirit on the rocky heart of the hearer, he breaks through the hardness and transforms it into a heart of flesh. He gives the hearer a new heart. In other words, he is born again.

The Holy Spirit only saves through the ministry of a spoken word—the gospel—the message of Jesus' life, death and resurrection.

23 …since you have been born again, not of perishable seed but of imperishable, through the living and abiding word of God; 24 for

"All flesh is like grass
and all its glory like the flower of grass.
The grass withers,
and the flower falls,
25 but the word of the Lord remains forever."

And this word is the good news that was preached to you.
(1 Peter 1:23-25)

All the components of our salvation are contained in this passage. We have regeneration (born again). We have the means of regeneration in the word (the gospel). And we have the proclamation of this gospel.

This is why all conversion stories share a common feature. They usually begin with some sort of indifference toward God. But then we'll hear something like, "But then I listened to a sermon…" or "I picked up a Bible tract…" or "I was reading a Bible that my Grandma gave me, and then I believed in Jesus."

All salvation stories have this moment where the truth about God in Jesus is understood with their mind in words and immediately received in their heart. Paul says something similar in Romans 10:17.

17 So faith comes from hearing, and hearing through the word of Christ. (Romans 10:17)

A Needed Assurance

Some may take issue with the Holy Spirit's regenerating work because it may somehow undermine our free agency. But have we considered that the Holy Spirit's work of regeneration may in fact be the very assurance we need in our Christian walk?

How often do we gravitate toward doubting our salvation based upon our delinquencies rather than on the Holy Spirit's delivering power? Could it be that we are relying on our free agency to keep us in the faith rather than the Holy Spirit who has brought us into faith?

Paul tells us in Ephesians that this work of the Holy Spirit is "guaranteed" for us. And we can rest assured that if he has brought us into faith, he will keep us in faith as well.

> 13 In him you also, when you heard the word of truth, the gospel of your salvation, and believed in him, were sealed with the promised Holy Spirit, 14 who is the guarantee of our inheritance until we acquire possession of it, to the praise of his glory. (Ephesians 1:13-14)

When we "heard the word of truth, the gospel of our salvation, and believed in him," God put our name in the book of life and firmly sealed it with an unbreakable seal, only to be opened on that final day when we cash in our inheritance.

The God Who Desires to Save

In basking in God's saving work, I hope that we better understand the character and nature of God and his desire to save. Oh, how we need to hear these wonderful truths of God's love and saving work through the gospel of Jesus Christ. This gospel is our lifeline as Christians. Paul says in Romans 1:16,

> 16 For I am not ashamed of the gospel, for it is the power of God for salvation to everyone who believes... (Romans 1:16)

The gospel isn't just for that one time event when we may have raised our hand and walked down a church aisle toward the front to make a decision for Christ. The gospel is for everyday life. It is God's power for today, to save us in this very moment, and secure for us an inheritance that no one can take away.

And while it may be that we sometimes live with uncertainty of God's love for us because of our occasional straying into unrighteousness, we can trust that the blood of Jesus is sufficient to "cleanse us from all unrighteousness." (1 John 1:9) Here's the bottom line: *God knows how poor our performance really is.* And in spite of that he still welcomes us home. He loves us with a love so deep that it cannot depend on our performance. It's a love bought with the blood of Jesus Christ, his Son.[2]

Pillar 7 Endnotes

[1] Dustin Kensrue "Son of David"

[2] There is a sense in which the love of God is unconditional, in that we can do nothing to gain more of his love. He gives it freely without conditions on our part. But this type of love—the love by which he loves us—was not purely unconditional. The condition by which we experience this love is the blood of Jesus his Son. It took a death to purchase this unique and special love that he dispenses on his people.

Pillar 8
Satan

Affirmation

Regarding Satan, we believe he is a powerful being [1] who was created by God [2] and consigned to reign over this present world [3]. His work includes destroying [4], murdering [5], deceiving [6], and accusing [7] humanity, constantly opposing God, while remaining under God's sovereign control [8].

[1] Revelation 12:4-9; [2] Ezekiel 28:12-16; [3] 1 John 5:19;
2 Corinthians 4:4; [4] 1 Peter 5:8; [5] John 8:44; [6] John 8:44;
[7] Zechariah 3:1; [8] Job 1:6-12

We believe that for those who have placed their faith in Jesus and his redemptive work on their behalf, Satan has lost his condemning power [1] and at the appointed time, he will meet his final doom, being cast into the lake of fire forever [2].

[1] Colossians 2:15; John 12:31; [2] Jude 6-7; Revelation 20:10

Satan

We briefly introduced the Devil in the previous pillar, showing how he conspires with our unbelief to blind our minds from seeing the glory of Christ. But there is more to this creature. We simply can't assume that we all hold the same understanding of Satan.[1] Therefore, we've dedicated this pillar to the exploration of our adversary as we find him in *Scripture*.

A Scale of Beliefs

We've already seen that one of the names of our adversary is "the god of this world." We all know him better as the Devil. But there are a number of beliefs about him, of which there seems to be two prominent extremes, with a smattering of various understandings in between.

On one hand, some believe there is no Devil. In post-modern, humanistic worldviews, belief in the existence of Satan is not all that popular. It would be no surprise to hear that an educated western grad student would view those who believe in the existence of such a creature as simple-minded folks. To them, believing in a creature wearing a red robe, with two-horns and a pitchfork is just as absurd as believing in unicorns. So that's one end of the scale—the skeptics.

On the other extreme, there are those who attribute too much power to the Devil, as though every evil was initiated and executed by him. If a loved one gets sick, or a pastor commits adultery, the devil did it. In this view, too much influence is ascribed to him, as though he were at the same level of God. Consequently, this evokes fear in these people.

But Jesus commands us, "Do not fear those who kill the body, but cannot kill the soul. Rather, fear him who can destroy both soul and body in hell." (Matthew 10:28) The only person that we ought to fear is God himself, after all, God is all-powerful and Satan is not.

So, with the spectrum of skepticism and "over-belief" we find it necessary that our affirmation presents a careful, biblical approach to our understanding of Satan. Our statement begins with, "Regarding Satan, we believe he is a powerful being…"

Satan: A Powerful Being

Let's start with the name for the Devil—Satan. *Satan* is a Hebrew term found throughout the Old Testament, which means "accuser." (Zechariah 3:1-2) This is Satan's main work—to accuse the guilty. There will be more on this later. But for now, we must recognize that this is his name, because he is a person who acts with this intent.

Satan is a being who has intent. He is not an impersonal force. He is not a euphemism for evil. He is a creature that God himself created. And because he was created, he too, has limitations. Satan is not eternal. He wasn't always in existence like the Father, Son, and Holy Spirit. There is a stark Creator/creature distinction.

With this distinction between God and Satan, this automatically puts him in a place of complete inferiority to God. But though he is finite, and a creature, *The Bible* also teaches that he does possess peculiar power. John paints a vivid picture of the Devil in Revelation 12:4-9.

4 His tail swept down a third of the stars of heaven and cast them to the earth. And the dragon stood before the woman who was about to give birth, so that when she bore her child he might devour it. 5 She gave birth to a male child, one who is to rule all the nations with a rod of iron, but her child was caught up to God and to his throne, 6 and the woman fled into the wilderness, where she has a place prepared by God, in which she is to be nourished for 1,260 days. 7 Now war arose in heaven, Michael and his angels fighting against the dragon. And the dragon and his angels fought back, 8 but he was defeated, and there was no longer any place for them in heaven. 9 And the great dragon was thrown down, *that ancient serpent, who is called the devil and Satan, the deceiver of the whole world*—he was thrown down to the earth, and his angels were thrown down with him. (Revelation 12:4-9)

John tells us that the *ancient serpent* is so powerful that he swept a third of the stars out of heaven. And we know that John is referring to Satan when he speaks of the ancient serpent because he identifies him by name in verse 9. What this tells us is that although he is finite, this creature also has tremendous power—enough to bring a third of the heavens down.

Consigned to Reign Over This Present World

The Bible also teaches that the Devil has reign over the present world. He hasn't been banished from it—at least not yet.

19 We know that we are from God, and the whole world lies in the power of the evil one. (1 John 5:19)

The *god of this world* (2 Corinthians 4:4) has a certain amount of power, authority, and influence in this world that he uses to work for destruction. Our statement continues with "His work includes destroying, murdering, deceiving, and accusing humanity…" All of his work reeks of disastrous evil.

Satan is a Destroyer

8 Be sober-minded; be watchful. Your adversary the devil prowls around like a roaring lion, *seeking someone to devour.* (1 Peter 5:8)

Satan is a Murderer

44 You are of your father the devil, and your will is to do your father's desires. *He was a murderer from the beginning*, and does not stand in the truth, because there is no truth in him. (John 8:44)

Satan is a Liar

44 When he lies, he speaks out of his own character, for he is a liar and the father of lies. (John 8:44)

Satan is an Accuser

1 Then he showed me Joshua the high priest standing before the angel of the LORD, and Satan standing at his right hand to accuse him. (Zechariah 3:1)

Opposing God

If we were to write down Satan's mission statement, it would be: "The devil exists to oppose God." Our statement reads that he is "constantly opposing God, though he remains under His sovereign control." Satan is everything that God isn't. Satan works against everything that God works for. He is dead-set on this mission.

Now, I understand that while reading about his power, we may feel a certain amount of fear creeping up within us. "Perhaps Satan has my number." This is the danger of the latter extreme.

But it's here that we must remember that while he is all of those things, *Satan is not sovereign.* Yes, he may have reign over this world, but he doesn't have total reign. There is one who is above his power and authority—God himself. Job demonstrates this hierarchy and just how powerless the devil is in light of God.

6 Now there was a day when the sons of God came to present themselves before the LORD, and Satan also came among them. 7 The LORD said to Satan, "From where have you come?" Satan answered the LORD and said, "From going to and fro on the earth, and from walking up and down on it." 8 And the LORD said to Satan, "Have you considered my servant Job, that there is none like him on the earth, a blameless and upright man, who fears God and turns away from evil?"

9 Then Satan answered the LORD and said, "Does Job fear God for no reason? 10 Have you not put a hedge around him and his house and all that he has, on every side? You have blessed the work of his hands, and his possessions have increased in the land. 11 But stretch out your hand and touch all that he has, and he will curse you to your face." 12 And the LORD said to Satan, "Behold, all that he has is in your hand. Only against him do not stretch out your hand." So Satan went out from the presence of the LORD. (Job 1:6-12)

The author of Job shows us that Satan operates only where God permits. I've heard it said somewhere, "Satan is on a leash." He can only go as far as God says, but no further.

Because the devil's work of destroying, murdering, deceiving and accusing is under the sovereign control of God, all that he seeks to destroy eventually works for God's purposes and his own glory. (cf. Genesis 50:20)

Lost Condemning Power

What this means for us as the people of God bought with the blood of Christ, is that we are safe and secure in God's loving hand. God has us firmly in his grip. (John 10:28-29) Our statement says, "We believe that for those who have placed their faith in Jesus and his redemptive work on their behalf, Satan has lost his condemning power."

So, in light of this, let's return to the name—Satan. *Satan* means "accuser". This is an appropriate designation for him. One of his main activities is rubbing a man's sins in his face. He takes their record of sins and reminds them before the Judge of the extent of their crimes. He accuses. And often his claims are not untrue. Satan takes our sin (including the sin of unbelief) and he holds it before God so that God can rightfully condemn us to death. He would say with seething contempt, something like,

> "Judge, look at how selfish, proud and arrogant this man has acted toward his wife and children. Look at his record: Abuse, complacency, adultery, and lie after lie to cover them all up. This man deserves death. Condemn him! He's guilty!"

The result of Satan's accusing work is despair. How often do we feel despair when we sin? Either we try and clean ourselves up, then feel the weight of our failure, or we surrender to our sinful passions knowing that any effort we make is futile. And so we despair in our sin.

But it's a different story for the children of God. Jesus has cleansed us of all our sins (1 John 1:9) and delivered us from the condemnation that we rightfully deserved. So, when Satan draws his accusatory weapon, he pulls the trigger to find there are no bullets in the chamber.

The Courtroom

Imagine this scenario: Satan is standing as the prosecutor in the God's heavenly courtroom. And day and night, he hurls accusations at us before God. He would say something like:

"That man is guilty! He's guilty! Look at these papers, Judge! Page after page after page, littered with his treacherous crimes against you! How can you ever acquit such a man? If you were to exonerate him, you would be just as wicked as him. Condemn him! He deserves it and you know it!"

Perhaps he would wrap up his closing statement with 1 Corinthians 6:9-10.

"9 Or do you not know that the unrighteous will not inherit the kingdom of God? ...neither the sexually immoral, nor idolaters, nor adulterers, nor men who practice homosexuality, 10 nor thieves, nor the greedy, nor drunkards, nor revilers, nor swindlers will inherit the kingdom of God.
(1 Corinthians 6:9-10)

The accuser has made his case. His indictment has been fully presented. And the Judge turned to us to say, "What's your defense?"

And there we would sit, with eyes lowered, slouched over the defendant's table under the weight of despair and guilt. The prosecutor was right. What could we say? Our rap sheet was spot on, and everyone knew it. All that's left is a desperate plea from a man at the end of his rope. "Have mercy on me, O, Judge, a sinner?" (Luke 18:13)

But it was in that moment that a lone voice echoed throughout the courtroom chambers from another man who approached the bench saying, "Judge, greater love has no one than this, that a man would lay down his life for his friends. And that defendant is my friend." (cf. John 15:13)

This other man then grabbed those pages from the prosecutor's hands, full of our treacherous crimes, and wadded them up, held them close to his heart, and exited the courtroom where he climbed a lonely hill to be condemned on a wooden cross. It was on that day our record of debt died with that man—Jesus Christ. Paul says in Colossians 2:13-15,

> 13 And you, who were dead in your trespasses and the uncircumcision of your flesh, God made alive together with him, having forgiven us all our trespasses, 14 *by canceling the record of debt that stood against us with its legal demands.* This he set aside, nailing it to the cross. 15 *He disarmed the rulers* and authorities and put them to open shame, by triumphing over them in him. (Colossians 2:13-15)

The Son of God has taken all our record of debt, put them on his body, nailed them to the cross, and the Judge has exonerated us. And with a loud voice, he has pronounced two verdicts. "Not guilty," and, "He is righteous!" The Accuser lost his case.

> 1 There is therefore now no condemnation for those who are in Christ Jesus. (Romans 8:1)

The Prosecution now has nothing in his hands except a blank sheet of paper. Satan's accusatory weapon has been dismantled. He's shooting blanks. What power does he have left? What weapon formed against us will prosper? (Isaiah 54:17)

Final Doom

If Satan destroys, God builds. If he kills, God raises up. If he deceives, God brings to light. If he accuses, God declares, "Righteous." He is a serpent who has been defanged—an accuser with no accusations left. And his destructive work will come to end when he is finally destroyed.

Our affirmation concludes, "at the appointed time, he will meet his final doom, being cast into the lake of fire forever." The Apostle John, in seeing the finality of human history revealed by God, describes Satan's destruction in Revelation 20:10.

> 10 and the devil who had deceived them was thrown into the lake of fire and sulfur where the beast and the false prophet were, and they will be tormented day and night forever and ever. (Revelation 20:10)

Yes, Satan is real. Yes, he is powerful. Yes, he is out to destroy us. But we need not fear our adversary. He has no power over our Father in heaven, and our Father has secured us in Christ. The Devil's wounds are only a sting. We are in the grip of God. The most that Satan can do is kill us—but even then, "neither death nor life…will be able to separate us from the love of God in Christ Jesus our Lord." (Romans 8:38)

I pray that our hearts would sing the praises of Jesus Christ who has fully purchased us, our record of debt, and declared us righteous before our accuser.

"Behold the man upon a cross
My sin upon His shoulders
Ashamed, I hear my mocking voice
Call out among the scoffers
It was my sin that held Him there
Until it was accomplished
His dying breath has brought me life
I know that it is finished"[2]

Pillar 8 Endnotes

[1] I will use "Satan" and "The Devil" interchangeably. "Satan" is another name given to the Devil in scripture. Satan is Hebrew (שָׂטָן) meaning "one who accuses". (1 Chronicles 21:1; Job 1:6-9; Zechariah 3:1-2)

[2] Stuart Townend, "How Deep the Father's Love for Us"

Pillar 9
The Church

Affirmation

Regarding the universal Church, we believe that she is comprised of all those who possess a persevering faith in Christ[1], both in generations past, present and future. These are the saints of God who were called out of the world and into fellowship with Him [2], thus overcoming the world[3] with Christ Jesus as her head [4].

[1] Hebrews 7:25, Ephesians 2:8-9, Revelation 5:9; [2] Ephesians 1:3-4;

[3] 1 John 5:4-5; [4] Colossians 1:18, Ephesians 1:22

Regarding the local church, we believe that God has commanded her, for her joy, to regularly gather together in congregational worship [1], devoting themselves to the Word of God, prayer, the ministry of fellowship [2], in addition to the biblical ordinances of water baptism [3] and participation of the Lord's Table [4].

[1] 1 Corinthians 16:19; Hebrews 10:24-25; [2] Acts 2:42;

Colossians 3:16; [3] Matthew 28:19; [4] 1 Corinthians 11:23-26

Regarding the gifts of the local church, we believe that the Holy Spirit has dispensed on every saint different gifts for worship, the common good of the church body [1], and for the advancement of the gospel [2], to the glory of God among the nations[3].

[1] Ephesians 4:11-14; Romans 12:4-8; [2] Romans 10:15;

[3] 1 Peter 2:9; 1 Peter 4:11; Mark 16:15

Universal Church

What do we mean when we say, "universal Church"? First, we should be careful to not confuse the word "universal" with "universalism". Universalism is the false teaching that affirms that everyone is, or eventually will be, a part of Jesus' Church. We do not adhere to that doctrine.

When we say, "universal Church" we're referring to the entirety of God's assembly that reaches beyond time and location, denomination and race. We do not believe that we, as *Redeemer Fellowship*, are the only true people of God, as some religions or sects teach for themselves. Yes, we are in fact a church, but we are not *the* Church—capital "C". Those who belong to the Church of Jesus extend far beyond our humble congregation in both time and geography.

The writers of the Apostles' Creed likewise wanted to include this concept of God's universal Church by writing, "We believe in the holy Catholic Church." The writers of this creed were not thinking of "Catholic" in terms of denomination, but in terms of universal Christianity—which is why some have changed the creed to "We believe in the holy *Christian* Church."

The Church of Jesus Christ is comprised of a wide array of people—young and old, rich and poor, from generations past to present, and global.

The Church as "She"

Our statement continues with, "…we believe that *she*…" Now let's pause here. Notice the feminine pronoun.

All throughout *The Bible*—from Old Testament Israel, to the New Testament Church—*The Bible* describes the people of God most commonly in feminine terms. Old Testament Israel and the New Testament Church are often described as the bride of God himself—signifying both the masculine aspects of God, and the feminine aspects of his chosen people. So in our use of the feminine pronoun, our aim is to highlight the biblical aspect of the Church as feminine—we belong to God himself as his beloved bride.

> 5 your Maker is your husband,
> the LORD of hosts is his name;
> and the Holy One of Israel is your Redeemer, (Isaiah 54:5)

> 25 Husbands, love your wives, as Christ loved the church and gave himself up for her... (Ephesians 5:25)

Persevering Faith

We also state that the Church "is comprised of all who possess a persevering faith in Christ..." The last clause—faith in Christ—should come as no surprise at this point. We have repeatedly emphasized faith in Christ throughout the entire affirmation. But we should direct our attention to the word "persevering."

By using "persevering" we want to qualify "saving faith." This is important because there are different types of "faith," as James indicates in his letter in chapter 2. There are phony faiths that take on all shapes and sizes, and then there is a genuine faith—a saving faith.

Jesus shows us what a phony faith looks like in his parable of the sower. He says in Matthew 13:20-21.

"20 As for what was sown on rocky ground, this is the one who hears the word and immediately *receives it with joy*, 21 yet he has no root in himself, but endures for a while, and when tribulation or persecution arises on account of the word, immediately he falls away." (Matthew 13:20-21)

We can see that in this parable, this person receives the word of God with joy. This means that he has heard the gospel and was happy about all that he heard. And by all appearances, it seemed that he was ready to grow. But that was just an aberration. While there may have been a sprig budding from the ground, there proved to be no root to secure him when trouble arose. Perhaps a strong wind came along and started tearing him from the ground he was planted in. Eventually, he fell away and proved that his faith was disingenuous. The Apostle John describes it like this,

19 They went out from us, but they were not of us; for if they had been of us, they would have continued with us.
(1 John 2:19)

We should notice that both Jesus and John's emphasis is not on how we begin our faith, but how we finish it. This is why we use the word "persevere". A persevering faith is the type that doesn't fall away. It continues and presses on in the hardship. Paul writes,

21 And you, who once were alienated and hostile in mind, doing evil deeds, 22 he has now reconciled in his body of flesh by his death, in order to present you holy and blameless and above reproach before him, 23 *if indeed you continue in the faith*, stable and steadfast, not shifting from the hope of the gospel that you heard, which has been proclaimed in all creation under heaven, and of which I, Paul, became a minister. (Colossians 1:21-23)

1 Now I would remind you, brothers, of the gospel I preached to you, which you received, in which you stand, 2 and by which you are being saved, *if you hold fast* to the word I preached to you—unless you believed in vain. (1 Corinthians 15:1-2)

Persevering Faith and Eternally Secure

At this point some of us may feel a conflict stirring within. On the one hand, we hear the necessity and urgency to persevere in the Christian walk. But on the other hand, it may also seem that the "guarantee" of salvation, promised by the Holy Spirit, is in jeopardy. The question may go something like this:

"I thought you said that the Holy Spirit guarantees my salvation and that all my sins—past, present, and future—are forgiven, yet you are also saying that unless my faith perseveres to the end I won't be saved? So which is it?"

This is a good question and one that *The Bible* addresses. As we open up the *Scriptures*, we find that there are continually these two paradigms. 1) God is working. 2) The saints are working. On one hand we are guaranteed by the Lord Jesus that:

"39 This is the will of him who sent me, that *I should lose nothing of all that he has given me, but raise it up on the last day.*" (John 6:39)

We can clearly see that coming to the faith and persevering in faith are both God's work and guarantee. Yet we also see that *The Bible* commands us to "hold fast" and "continue in the faith."

What the biblical authors are doing is showing that there is a particular faith that encompasses both of these paradigms. Persevering faith is given and cultivated by God. At the same time, it is a faith so unique that it necessitates growth. It's like a healthy orange tree that produces healthy oranges. It's not that the oranges *make* the tree an orange tree. The oranges *prove* that the tree is a living orange tree. So it is with faith. The perseverance (our work) is the proof of genuine faith (God's work).

Persevering faith doesn't put on a good face, sign a card that says, "I accepted Jesus in my heart" and then continues in sin. That is a dead faith, as James 2:17 says. The Apostle John says that person is a liar. (1 John 1:6) But the faith that God gives will prove to be genuine as it is a faith that perseveres in love for God and love for others.

Throughout Generations

Our affirmation continues, "both in generations past, present and future." The point of this statement, as it relates to persevering faith, is to highlight that salvation extends beyond one group of people in any particular time. This is a reminder that God is the redeemer of all types of people, throughout all generations.

Salvation has come to his Church in first century Palestine, just as it has come to those in Europe during the Reformation. The power of God in the gospel of Jesus Christ has come to communist China in the late 20th century, just as it has come to us in 2018. Saving faith has no bounds on people groups, language, geography, or time. God is the redeemer of all men.

Called Out

The first portion of this affirmation concludes with, "These are the saints of God who were called out of the world and into fellowship with Him, thus overcoming the world with Christ Jesus as her head."

Persevering faith has a certain face. When God saves us, he calls us out of the world. This means that our citizenship changes from something that was once familiar and safe to something that is completely other and outer. When we believed in Jesus, we became citizens of a new land. And one of the effects of this immigration, is that we feel a little out of place. After all, we were once citizens of darkness, but now of light. We talk differently now. We value different things. We are grafted into a deeper heritage. We are, in fact, aliens and strangers. (Hebrews 11:13) We are unsettled pilgrims on our way home to the heavenly city that we were destined for.

4 [God] chose us in him before the foundation of the world, that we should be holy and blameless before him. (Ephesians 1:4)

9 But you are a chosen race, a royal priesthood, a holy nation, a *people for his own possession*, that you may proclaim the excellencies of him who called you out of darkness into his marvelous light. (1 Peter 2:9)

What About Now?

God has claimed us as his own possession so that we would come into his new glories as princes dressed in his royal robes and rule with him as those who have overcome the world. We are pilgrims who have been promised victory over the world as we head to our final destination.

Now, some might say at this point,

> "Well that's fine and good for the future. I love the idea of ruling with Jesus, but what about now? What are we to do in the meantime? Don't get me wrong. I am excited for that day when there are no more tears, pain, or death, and we are ruling the world with Jesus in our new home. But what about now?"

While it's true that we are citizens of a new world, we also must remember that we have not yet arrived. We still journey through this world with all its aches, pains, and allures. Despite what the prosperity preachers propagate, our pilgrim life is not promised to be prosperous in health and wealth. We are rather promised trouble. (John 16:33) And these worldly troubles, no doubt, have been the downfall for many walking the Christian path.

We know how easy it is to despair when all we see is rough terrain with no sight of this "narrow gate" that we are commanded to enter. (Matthew 7:13-14) But it's here that God relieves our despair and gives us strength to rise up and walk. How?

God has give us promises that have proven to be the potency that enables us to stand when our knees are weak, ensuring that we have the legs to stay the course.

Run the Plays

I like sports. So indulge this pastor his one "token sports analogy." Let's imagine this scenario:

Imagine that the owner of a football league organized an exhibition game between two teams with the winning team taking home a notable cash prize. And guess what? You're the quarterback for one of those teams.

Now supposed the owner brings you aside and says, "Don't worry! I've arranged that you and your team win the game. Don't walk out on me. Trust me. Everyone will benefit. All I need for you to do is run the plays. Just run the plays!"

We should ignore the fact that this owner is doing something immoral, and probably illegal. The analogy is not about the owner. Rather, it's about you, the quarterback. Normally, given the opponent, you would despair in playing the game. They're bigger, faster, and meaner than any of your guys.

But imagine how differently you would play knowing for certain that the outcome of the game is set. Normally, in your despair, you would take a snap and throw the ball away, in fear of getting hit play after play. But this time, because of the owners promise, you won't throw the ball away. You're going to do exactly what the owner told you to do. "Just run the plays!"

His promise would have a way of pulling out the confidence that you would need to play the game well. And you would run those plays with toughness and fortitude because you would know that the outcome is already secured.

The opponents may think that they've got a shot at winning. But what they don't know is that the owner has hired the refs, the coaches, and some new star athletes for your team to guarantee a win. From the very first snap of the ball and every play that follows, you would play like the champions that you already were.

This is how God's promises act for us in the present. Uncertainty of the future can often keep us from running the plays. We may see that the odds are stacked against us. The task is too great. Our opponent is bigger. They are fiercer. They have more grit. They even have a winning record. We may see all of that and think, "I can't win." And so the result is that we don't even try. We give up. Why even continue, right?

Overcome

But we are God's children. We know how it ends. In calling us out of darkness and into light, God has already secured victory for us —his people. He has purchased, with the blood of his Son, victory over sin, death, the devil and all the forces of this present darkness. We see this precious promise heralded over our tired souls in 1 John 5:4-5.

> 4 For everyone who has been born of God *overcomes* the world. And this is the *victory* that has *overcome* the world—our faith. 5 Who is it that *overcomes* the world except the one who believes that Jesus is the Son of God? (1 John 5:4-5)

The word "overcome" in the ESV is the same word for "victory" (*nike*).[1] John is emphasizing the *nike* that we as children of God have already obtained. The victory is secured. John teaches us that Satan, sin, and death are not ultimate. And our faith has become the agent that conquers the evil one and dismantles all of his schemes.

If we sin, we have an advocate. If Satan accuses, Jesus declares righteous. If we die, God resurrects. And so it is that all the weapons employed by the enemy have proven powerless by our faith in Jesus, the true heir and firstborn Son of God. His is the only heir-support we need. He's guaranteed victory for us already, as we journey to the heavenly city by which we have not yet arrived.

With Christ as Her Head

Before Jesus ended his small group meeting with prayer, he reminded his disciples of this victory. But before this, he shared with them an unpleasant reality—one that I just alluded to. He says,

"In the world, you will have tribulation. But take heart, I have overcome the world." (John 16:33)

"One thing is guaranteed for you disciples. I'm not guaranteeing your dream job. I'm not promising you a long life, with good health, and a big family. I'm not ensuring that you will have lands, servants, and wealth. *I'm guaranteeing trouble*. Your life will be hard."

We would do well in our day to remember Jesus' promise of tribulation. This is the pilgrim's path. It will not be easy. Jesus has promised a full garage. But this isn't where he ends. An anchor of hope is found in the second half. He commands, "Take heart. I have conquered the world."

This fact—this reality—becomes the power that enables his people to persevere when inevitable trouble arises. Our prince has already ridden into battle, secured the field, and disarmed the rulers. Our protector has guaranteed his protection, rescued his bride, and now is bringing her home to his palace. We can almost hear Jesus say, "Join me in this victory. I will lead you. I will guide you. I will save you. I will protect you. Remember! I am your husband, and you are my bride. I am your God and you are my people."

Head over His Church

This is why our statement caps the first portion of this pillar with Jesus being our head. He has secured a victory for us already, and promised his protection for us as we war against the evil terrain on our pilgrimage. He is our covering.

18 And he is the head of the body, the church. (Colossians 1:18)

22 And he put all things under his feet and gave him as head over all things to the church… (Ephesians 1:22)

This is our identity as the Church—called by God into his fellowship, under the headship of Christ, while obtaining victory with him over sin, evil, the devil and the forces of darkness.

The Church's Worship

Our affirmation now focuses on the implications of this victory with Christ as our head. How do we, as individuals, function within a larger, specific church body?

"Regarding the local church, we believe that God has commanded her to regularly gather together in congregational worship."

It has now become normal in the American Church to practice Christianity in an exclusively private manner. This is no surprise, being that we are a culture that highly values individuality. This, coupled with the rapid advancement in technology,[2] has driven us more into isolation.[3] It's not uncommon to hear someone say, "I don't go to church. I worship God in nature. I feel the most connected to him when I'm by myself in his creation."

While I don't want to discredit a person feeling healthier when taking a break from the busy-ness and noise of the modern day, this feeling of profound worship does not mean that this is a "church" by any biblical definition.

The *Scriptures* teach otherwise. While private Christian disciplines like prayer, and God's Word, are vital, there is no such thing as Christianity lived "*privately*". We will search in vain to find this concept ever taught in *The Bible*. Yes. It is important that we have a personal relationship with our Lord, but it is equally important, and vital, that our relationship not be personal *only*.

> 24 And let us consider *how to stir up one another* to love and good works, 25 *not neglecting to meet together*, as is the habit of some, but *encouraging one another*, and all the more as you see the Day drawing near. (Hebrews 10:24-25)

It's even more evident how imperative the gathering together of the saints is for the author of Hebrews in the verse that follows.

> 26 For if we go on sinning deliberately after receiving the knowledge of the truth, there no longer remains a sacrifice for sins… (Hebrews 10:26)

When the author says, "For," he is giving the very basis for the importance of meeting together, which is, "if we go on sinning deliberately." In the author's mind, this means that the gathering of the saints is the very means that protects us against deliberately sinning. In other words, faith lived *together* protects faith dying *alone*. Living life in community is one of the most effective ways to guard our hearts against developing patterns of deliberate sin—which then lead to falling away.

The New Testament Church understood this, so much that many would risk their lives for the sake of being together. They didn't have this concept of privatized Christianity. They were bonded by the blood of Christ, the word of their testimony, and their suffering together for the sake of Christ.

Word & Prayer

Now, what did they do when they gathered together? Did they just hang out? While "hanging out" may be fun and even important, we see rather, that the early church was intentional with their worship together. Our statement says that the Church is to gather together in worship by… "devoting themselves to the Word of God and prayer…" It's here that we take our cues from the early church.

One of the earliest accounts of congregational worship is described in Acts, following Pentecost.

42 And they devoted themselves to the apostles' teaching and the fellowship, to the breaking of bread and the prayers. (Acts 2:42)

The earliest church regularly practiced gathering together to listen to the Apostles' teaching and pray. These are the "vertical" aspects of corporate worship, meaning that instruction and prayer are a practice directed upward—toward God.

Both teaching and prayer are the nuts and bolts of Christian worship. The Word of God is to be proclaimed and prayer is to saturate our time together.

We have much to learn from the early church, in this regard. Our churches need more faithfulness in prayer and the Word of God. Our churches don't need more comedian pastors, great communicators, story-tellers, or orators with all their musings. The Church needs to return to these pillars that the early church stood upon—robust teaching coupled with a deep prayer life.

Fellowship

But as vital as these vertical aspects are in congregational worship, we also recognize that they are not the only aspects. Acts also describes a horizontal aspect.

> And they devoted themselves to the apostles' teaching and *the fellowship, to the breaking of bread* and the prayers. (Acts 2:42)

Our statement identifies the fellowship and breaking of bread as "the ministry of fellowship…" The Church's collective worship honors God not only when our focus is upward—directed toward him in teaching and prayer—but also outward—directed toward one another. Our worship is bi-directional, taking the Godward focus and bending it outward to one another. We take our love for God, and apply it by loving the church body.

This is "fellowship". Fellowship is a concentrated effort, when gathering together, to hear from God in one another by exercising our spiritual gifts (more on this later), praying, eating together, and singing psalms, hymns, and spiritual songs. (See Ephesians 5:18-19)

Ordinances

Now, there's one more aspect to the Church's gathering together that we see demonstrated in *The Bible*. In addition to teaching, prayer, and fellowship, we also see that the early church made a practice to obey what Jesus had commanded the Church. These commands are commonly referred to as "biblical ordinances."

Jesus gave his Church two ordinances to continue to practice throughout the generations. What are they? We conclude our statement with, "in addition to the *biblical ordinances* of water baptism and participation in the Lord's Table."

The Lord Jesus commands his Church to practice two things—baptism and eating at the Lord's Table.

19 Go therefore and make disciples of all nations, *baptizing* them in the name of the Father and of the Son and of the Holy Spirit… (Matthew 28:19)

23 For I received from the Lord what I also delivered to you, that the Lord Jesus on the night when he was betrayed took bread, 24 and when he had given thanks, he broke it, and said, "This is my body which is for you. *Do this in remembrance of me.*" 25 In the same way also he took the cup, after supper, saying, "This cup is the new covenant in my blood. *Do this, as often as you drink it, in remembrance of me.*" (1 Corinthians 11:23-25)

Both of these ordinances are more than just commands. Often times we think of commandments as burdensome—just another thing to *do*. But Jesus never intended his commands to be a heavy burden. Rather, these ordinances become a blessing for his Church.[4]

Witnessing someone identifying with Jesus in his death and resurrection in baptism, and participating together in the bread and wine as symbols of Jesus' death have proven to be a tremendous of worship.

Putting it Together

When we put all of these components together—both the vertical aspects of the *Word of God* and prayer, coupled with the horizontal aspects of fellowship and biblical ordinances—we see the full spectrum of congregational worship. This is what the Church does, as described in *Scripture*, when they gather together.[5]

Gifts

These were the intentional practices that made up congregational worship when the saints gathered together at the beginning of the Christian Church. They have become for us the template that we both refer to and build upon.

But all of these aspects of congregational worship deal only with those practices when we gather together. The question remains: Does the Church have any responsibility outside of gathering together? What happens on the other five or six days of the week? Our statement continues with the gifts of the Holy Spirit.

> "Regarding the gifts of the local church, we believe that the Holy Spirit has dispensed on every saint different gifts for worship, the common good of the church body, and the advancement of the gospel, to the glory of God among the nations.

We know that Christianity is not just on Sunday. The Holy Spirit has given certain gifts to every believer so that they would exercise them when needed, "according to the measure of faith that God has assigned…" (Romans 12:3) for the good of the body.

These gifts include prophecy, service, teaching, encouraging, giving, leading, mercy, wisdom, knowledge, healing, miracles, discernment, tongues, and interpretation of tongues. (Romans 12; 1 Corinthians 12)

The implication is that we have a responsibility as individuals to one another at all times, not just on Sundays from 9:30am to 11:30am. With the Holy Spirit's power, given by God, we also have a responsibility to serve one another for the common good of the wider church body. In fact, this is how the Apostle Paul refers to the local church—as a person's body. He says,

> 14 For the body does not consist of one member but of many. 15 If the foot should say, "Because I am not a hand, I do not belong to the body," that would not make it any less a part of the body." (1 Corinthians 12:14-15)

Paul then continues by explaining his metaphor in verse 27.

> 27 Now you are the body of Christ and individually members of it. (1 Corinthians 12:27)

This very idea of a person belonging to a larger group of people, for the benefit of that people, flies in the face of consumerism —even in the Church. It seems normal vernacular to hear Christians say, "We're church-shopping." Is there anything more consumerist than shopping?

But the gifts of the Holy Spirit are intended to do the exact opposite—not to see what we can get out of a people, but what we can give to a people—to benefit them—to build them up and make them stronger where they had weaknesses. And so *The Bible* challenges us in this way:

"What gifts can I exercise for the common good of my church body?"

This is a question that we all should be asking.

The Church on Mission

While we recognize the responsibility we have to each other, outside of Sunday morning, we also recognize the responsibility we have to those beyond the walls of the Church—to the world. We not only desire the spiritual health of Christians—that they are sustained and empowered in the gospel of Jesus Christ—but we also desire that those who don't know Jesus come to a saving knowledge of him. Part of what it means to "make disciples" just as Jesus commanded, is to proclaim the message of Jesus Christ to the world with the hope that they would be saved. This is why our affirmation concludes with, "… the advancement of the gospel, and the glory of God among the nations."

Most of us are well acquainted with the commission given by Jesus in Matthew 28:19-20, as we've already seen.

> "19 Go therefore and make disciples of all nations, baptizing them in the name of the Father and of the Son and of the Holy Spirit, 20 teaching them to do all that I have commanded, and surely I am with you even to the end of the age." (Matthew 28:19-20)

We get a sense of *urgency* from our Lord, right before his ascension. There is a mission to accomplish—the glory of God spreading across the globe as more and more people believe in Jesus, and walk in obedience to him.

Notice that Jesus doesn't leave his Church purposeless, existing in a realm of relaxation, laughter, or leisure—as is so often believed by many. We are not commissioned by our Lord to stay in our homes—to build thicker walls and higher fences. We are called to "*Go!*" Jesus says to his Church, "*Go!*" And in case this mission seems unattainable, he reminds us that he has not left us ill equipped. He has also promised that he will be with us. Jesus promises in the gospel of Luke,

> "11 And when they bring you before the synagogues and the rulers and the authorities, do not be anxious about how you should defend yourself or what you should say, 12 for the Holy Spirit will teach you in that very hour what you ought to say." (Luke 12:11-12)

We have been equipped with the promise of God's power in the Holy Spirit to accomplish Jesus' mission. O what comfort and courage this brings us—the meek of the earth—the Church of Jesus Christ. We, who have seen the glory of God (John 1:14) are commissioned to proclaim that glory—the glory of what we've seen to the ends of the earth—the nations of the world—even at the cost of our lives. All of this is undergirded with the promise that God will be with us.

The Church

This is the Church. We are both pilgrims of the world and the precious bride of Christ. We are offspring of the Father and outsiders of the world. We are many members, and yet one body. We are disciples making disciples. We are the Church, called by God, to cover the earth with his glory "as the waters cover the sea." (Habakkuk 2:14)

> 11…in everything God may be glorified through Jesus Christ. To him belong glory and dominion forever and ever. Amen. (1 Peter 4:11)

Pillar 9 Endnotes

[1] This is where the famous shoe company got its name. Nike is Greek for "victory".

[2] Tony Reinke makes the observation in his book, "12 Ways Your Phone is Changing You" that "For manufacturers and marketers, human beings are best when they are alone, since individuals are forced to buy one consumer item each, whereas family or community members share…Technology's movement toward miniaturization serves this end by making personal electronics suitable for individual users. For today's carefully trained consumers, sharing is an intrusion on personal space." (Page 123) Tony Reinke, *12 Ways Your Phone is Changing You* (Wheaton, Illinois: Crossway, 2017), p. 123.

[3] There are even churches that promote their "online churches" where you can experience "church" without ever leaving your home. Hopefully after reading this, you will be able to articulate how an "online church" is no church at all.

[4] See Appendix A: Baptism. This document is a summary that we teach through with everyone who wants to be baptized in our church.

[5] Sunday morning has historically been the designated time for congregational worship. Given that all these components of congregational worship converge on Sunday morning, this day possesses a precious peculiarity. It is the Sabbath Day in practice. Therefore we regularly challenge our congregation to make preparations in their own heart the night before we come together on Sunday morning. We also challenge the congregation to make church attendance non-optional. This isn't to say that we require perfect attendance. Rather, we encourage them to regard our time together with the same esteem that Hebrews does—to regard our time as vital to our faith in Christ.

Pillar 10
The Return of Jesus

Affirmation

Regarding the return of Christ Jesus, we believe that the blessed hope of God's children [1] is that at the appointed time He will return to His world personally [2], physically [3] and suddenly [4] in power and magnificent glory [5].

[1] Titus 2:13-14; [2] Acts 1:9-11, Revelation 1:7;

[3] Mark 14:62; Philippians 3:20-21; [4] 1 Thessalonians 5:2-3;

[5] Luke 21:27

As to the last day, we believe that at His coming, God will bodily raise everyone from the dead.

Daniel 12:2; Acts 24:15; John 5:28-29; 1 Thessalonians 4:13-18;

2 Thessalonians 1:7-9

As to the non-elect, God will judge all who suppressed the truth in unrighteousness [1] and consequently consign them to eternal conscious misery in Hell [2].

[1] Romans 1:18 [2] Matthew 3:12b; 10:28; 18:8; 25:31-46; Mark 3:29;
Luke 16:26; Acts 17:31; Jude 12-13;
2 Thessalonians 1:9; Revelation 14:11; 19:3; 20:10, 15

As to the elect, [1] God will gather them into His consummated kingdom to share in His everlasting joy, in His presence[2] where they will reign with Jesus Christ forever in the New Heavens and New Earth [3].

[1] Matthew 3:12a, 24:30, 31; [2] Matthew 25:23, 46, John 3:16, 14:3,
1 Corinthians 15:22-24, 2 Timothy 4:1, Luke 22:28-30; [3] Matthew
19:29, Romans 8:17, 1 Corinthians 2:9,
Luke 22:29-30, 2 Timothy 2:12

The Return of Jesus

Our last pillar focuses on the Christian's future at the closing of history. It's no doubt that the return of the Christ has been taught in both the Old and New Testaments, yet many have denied it. This denial again proves the necessity to articulate our position regarding these fundamental Christian doctrines. So let's turn our attention toward this last pillar of hope—a hope that we will need—a hope that will carry us through the trouble in the world as we make our way home to the New Jerusalem.

We begin with Acts 1:9-11 where Luke records the ascension of Jesus after his resurrection. Luke writes,

> 9 And when he had said these things, as they were looking on, he was lifted up, and a cloud took him out of their sight. 10 And while they were gazing into heaven as he went, behold, two men stood by them in white robes, 11 and said, "Men of Galilee, why do you stand looking into heaven? This Jesus, who was taken up from you into heaven, *will come in the same way as you saw him go into heaven.*" (Acts 1:9-11)

I find it fascinating that these two men in white robes seem like everything is business as usual. They nonchalantly ask everyone, "Why are you looking up?"

"Oh, I don't know, maybe because our best friend—who, by the way, was executed a few weeks ago—was just standing right next to us and now he's pulled a David Blaine right into orbit. But sure, ask us what we're looking at? No big deal! Nothing to see here."

But the fact was, there was nothing to see there. The men were right. There was no time for Son-gazing—not while there remained a dark world aching for the light of the risen Christ.

Now, we should also notice that these two men didn't only ask them, "What are you looking at?" but they also gave Jesus' disciples a promise—the promise that Jesus would come back again. This very promise has become the blessed hope of all of God's children—of both you and I. And this is where are final pillar begins.

Our Blessed Hope

Our affirmation first identifies Jesus' coming as a "blessed hope" and for the believer it's a hope that we possess in the present. Human beings are creatures of hope. We all have longings—longing for certain things that we have not yet acquired. This is like a seven-year-old's longing on December 24th. His hope is that his longing will be satisfied with a gift under a tree on December 25th. Likewise, our hope is in a day that has yet to come, and in a person who was not found under a tree, but nailed to tree. (Galatians 3:13) It was there that he died and rose again so that we might also live with him. (Colossians 2:12) The Apostle Paul writes about our blessed hope of life in his letter to Titus.

> 12 training us to renounce ungodliness and worldly passions, and to live self-controlled, upright, and godly lives in the present age, 13 waiting for *our blessed hope*, the appearing of the glory of our great God and Savior Jesus Christ. (Titus 2:12-13)

Paul describes the Christian as waiting for a blessed hope. And what is this blessed hope? It's the appearing of Christ—our savior.

So, while it is that we hold fast to the truth of Jesus' life and death on our behalf, we also find the genesis of our hope in his resurrection and ascension. At his ascension, Jesus has taken his position at the Father's right hand, but has not taken his final rest. He's not settled into the throne. He's returned home only to gather his troops and arrive on the battlefield for one final engagement, where he will appear before everyone in magnificent glory.

So if Jesus is coming back again, as the two men said, and his return will be like his ascension, then in order to understand his return, we should examine his ascension. Let's look at how he left so we can know how he will return.

Personally and Physically

The ascension of Christ was not a magic show. God didn't perform an illusion in Jesus' resurrection and ascension. His ascension was not devoid of flesh, and now to be regarded as spiritualized within, as the Esoterics taught.[1] Nor was Jesus' body just a semblance of a man, like the Docetist taught.[2] The risen Christ was the same person he was when he walked the earth—a man with mind, body, and soul. Because we are told that he will return in the same way that he departed, we can expect that Jesus will return in his fullness of person and body.

Paul, in Philippians 3:20, and John in Revelation 1:7 both write specifically about Jesus' glorified body at his return.

20 But our citizenship is in heaven, and from it we await a Savior, the Lord Jesus Christ, 21 who will transform our lowly body to be like his glorious body, by the power that enables him

even to subject all things to himself. (Philippians 3:20-21)

7 Behold, he is coming with the clouds, and every eye will see him, even those who pierced him, and all tribes of the earth will wail on account of him. Even so. Amen. (Revelation 1:7)

Suddenly

Given this last verse we see that his appearance also comes suddenly. There are some false teachers presently, like the Jehovah's Witnesses, who teach that Jesus' return will be in a duration of time—starting in 1914 and moving until Armageddon. But *The Bible* teaches otherwise.

2 For you yourselves are fully aware that the day of the Lord will come like a thief in the night. 3 While people are saying, "There is peace and security," then sudden destruction will come upon them as labor pains come upon a pregnant woman, and they will not escape. (1 Thessalonians 5:2-3)

The comparison to a thief is important when understanding Jesus' second coming. A thief typically doesn't start his work in the twilight of Monday and gradually break into a house on Friday. He comes unexpected and quickly. And that is the way Christ will come.

But Christ also comes like labor pains to a pregnant woman. Mothers know what I'm talking about here. Unless induced, there is no formal announcement from the uterus requesting a convenient date to pencil in. They come unannounced.

And contractions not only come suddenly, but they also come

violently. Likewise, Jesus will not come stealth-like as some sort of cosmic ninja, but more like a S.W.A.T. team ramming down the front door. (Again, mothers know what I'm talking about.) Jesus will appear suddenly, and "in power and magnificent glory."

Power and Glory

Part of what differentiates his second coming from his first is this display of his power. Jesus prophesies about this very thing in Luke 21:7. He instructs his disciples:

> "27 And then they will see the Son of Man coming in a cloud with power and great glory." (Luke 21:27)

The sight will be one to behold, and one that will be frightening for many. There is no redoing the incarnation. Jesus will not come again in a lowly state, as the Rastafarians believe.[3] He has already fulfilled that role as the suffering servant. We now await his return, as one who...

> 9 ...shall break them with a rod of iron
> and dash them in pieces like a potter's vessel.
> (Psalm 2:9)

We await the return of the Righteous King. The Apostle John in his colorful language, describes for us with vivid terminology what his return will entail. There is a frightful nature to his power and glory.

11 Then I saw heaven opened, and behold, a white horse! The

one sitting on it is called Faithful and True, and in righteousness he judges and makes war. 12 *His eyes are like a flame of fire,* and on his head are many diadems, and he has a name written that no one knows but himself. 13 He is clothed in a robe dipped in blood, and the name by which he is called is *The Word of God.* 14 And the armies of heaven, arrayed in fine linen, white and pure, were following him on white horses. 15 *From his mouth comes a sharp sword* with which to strike down the nations, and he will rule them with a rod of iron. He will tread the winepress of the fury of the wrath of God the Almighty. 16 On his robe and on his thigh he has a name written, *King of kings and Lord of lords.* (Revelation 19:11-16)

This is the "power and magnificent glory" we are referring to in our affirmation. His appearance will be significant. And along with his appearance, there will also accompany significant events. This moves us into the second portion of our affirmation. We state, "As to the last day, we believe that at His coming, God will bodily raise everyone from the dead."

The Last Day

Many passages testify to the resurrection of the dead, but we want to focus on three—one from the Old Testament (Daniel), one from the Gospels (John), and one from Acts.

2 And many of those who sleep in the dust of the earth shall awake, some to everlasting life, and some to shame and everlasting contempt. (Daniel 12:2)

28 Do not marvel at this, for an hour is coming when all who are in the tombs will hear his voice 29 and come out, those who have done good to the resurrection of life, and those who have done evil to the resurrection of judgment. (John 5:28)

14 I worship the God of our fathers, believing everything laid down by the Law and written in the Prophets, 15 having a hope in God, which these men themselves accept, that there will be a resurrection of both the just and the unjust. (Acts 24:14-15)

These are only a few passages that teach that everyone will be raised on the final day. But we must ensure that we have a proper understanding of this resurrection. You'll also notice in these passages that we will be taken into only one of the two destinations. Yes, all will rise, but when raised, where will we go? Just because everyone is raised does not mean that everyone is raised to eternal life. So then what happens to those who do not go to eternal life? To answer this, let's first look at the two destinations.

Two Destinations

Daniel identifies one group entering into everlasting life while the other group enters into shame and contempt. John then identifies the two *groups* as, "those who do good," obtaining a "resurrection of life," while "those who do evil" obtain a "resurrection of judgment." In our most basic understanding, these two destinations have been referred to as heaven and hell. These are the only two destinations for every human being…for either the just or the unjust, as John puts it.

Two Groups

Now what about the two groups? The most remarkable account comes from another gospel. Matthew records Jesus illustrating his second coming as a process of separating sheep from goats.

> 31 "When the Son of Man comes in his glory, and all the angels with him, then he will sit on his glorious throne. 32 Before him will be gathered all the nations, and he will separate people one from another as a shepherd separates the sheep from the goats. 33 And he will place the sheep on his right, but the goats on the left. 34 Then the King will say to those on his right, 'Come, you who are blessed by my Father, inherit the kingdom prepared for you from the foundation of the world.'" (Matthew 25:31-34)

He continues in verse 41 with the goats.

41 "Then he will say to those on his left, 'Depart from me, you cursed, *into the eternal fire* prepared for the devil and his angels...' 46 And these will go away into *eternal punishment*, but the righteous into eternal life." (Matthew 25:41, 46)

Using the Term "Elect"

We have identified these two groups in our affirmation as the "elect" and "non-elect". Now before we take a closer look at these two groups, some may be wondering why we use the terminology of "elect" and "non-elect." For some, it may sound overly "Calvinistic" and therefore unnecessary.

Simply put, we use this terminology because *The Bible* does. In Matthew 24, which is one of Jesus' few teachings on the Last Day, he uses the word "elect". He says,

"31 And he will send out his angels with a loud trumpet call, and they will gather his *elect* from the four winds, from one end of heaven to the other." (Matthew 24:31)

And Jesus is not the only one who uses this term. Paul in 2 Timothy 2:10 and Romans 8:33 refers to those who belong to Christ as the "elect." So, given its biblical basis, especially as it relates to the second coming of Christ, it's an appropriate designation for this pillar. But this isn't the only reason we use this word.

In addition, the word "elect" communicates God's all-powerful hand in saving his people to the uttermost. (Hebrews 7:25) There is an undercurrent of confidence in God's ability to keep us, despite our wandering appetite. When God *elects* us, we have a certainty that the work he began in us, he will complete (Philippians 1:6) and he will see us through to the end. The word "elect" celebrates the sovereignty of God in our salvation and his ability to keep us. When we feel too weak to walk our troubled path, we know that God will carry those whom he has elected.

The Non-Elect

But let's now turn our attention toward the non-elect.[4] What is immediately noticeable with this group is that their destination is a horrific one. Paul describes the non-elect in Romans 1:18 as the "ungodly" and "unrighteous" who "suppress the truth in unrighteousness." And he shows us that the consequence of their suppression is the revealing of God's wrath. (See also John 3:36)

The Bible teaches us that there is no safety for anyone outside of Christ, both now, and in the future. Jesus appeared once to save us from God's wrath both in the "already" and the "not yet."

Now some may respond to this by saying, "Well, if his wrath is on me now, than his wrath doesn't seem so bad. I have a pretty good life." And it may, in fact, be a pleasant life…at least for now. The Lord has a strange way of using suffering to get our attention. He has a way of exercising his wrath so that we would turn from our sin. (Luke 13:4-5) So although things may be grand now, it likely will not remain that way. Pain afflicts us all.

But we should note that God's present wrath is not the only wrath there is. Our statement additionally says that there is a *future* judgment that awaits those who do not believe in the Son of God. Our affirmation reads, "…and consequently consign them to eternal conscious misery in Hell."

The Wrath of God

The word "consequence" means that God's wrath is deserved. Regarding rebels, God's wrath is not unwarranted. "The wages of sin is death…" (Romans 6:23) If we sow sin, we reap death. And a life of sowing sin not only reaps an earthly death, but an ongoing death beyond the grave.

Looking at Matthew 25:41, Jesus says that he will say to the disobedient goats,

> 41 'Depart from me, you cursed, *into the eternal fire* prepared for the devil and his angels…' 46 And these will go away into *eternal punishment.*" (Matthew 25:41, 46)

This is the consequence of the unrighteousness of the goats—a place of "eternal fire" and "eternal punishment".

Jesus minces no words when it comes to our eternal destiny —"cursed," "eternal," and "fire" as possible destinies, should instill in us a holy terror. This is why our affirmation states that it is an "eternal conscious misery."

Hell is a place, where many will be fully aware of their misery and pain—pain warranted from a life of rebellion against a holy God. The Apostle John refers to this as the "second death"—a death that is ongoing and eternal. (Revelation 21:8)

The Elect

Now what is the destination of the other group—the elect? Our statement concludes:

> "As to the elect, God will gather them into His consummated kingdom to share in His everlasting joy, in His presence where they will reign with Jesus Christ forever in the New Heavens and New Earth."

For the elect of God, his second coming is not a fearful burden but a blessed hope. The elect of God will never taste the bitterness of his wrath, either now or in hell. We will only taste the sweetness of his love. Looking at Matthew 24:31 again, Jesus says,

> "31 And he will send out his angels with a loud trumpet call, and they will gather his *elect* from the four winds, from one end of heaven to the other." (Matthew 24:31)

There are two things to note in this verse. The first is that God is the one gathering. We should not gloss over this too quickly. Before Jesus comes back on that terrifying day, we are reassured that God will first gather his own. It's an act of his saving grace once again. We are firmly secured in his sovereign hand.

The second thing to notice is that his people are not consigned to a specific geography. Jesus makes it a point to say that his people are not identified by ethnicity, heritage, or clan. He gathers them from all sides of the earth—indeed all who have put their trust in Christ.

Consummated Kingdom

The purpose of God gathering his elect is to bring them into his consummated kingdom. We use the word "consummated" to communicate the completed and finalized version of God's kingdom. It's the same kingdom that Jesus inaugurated at his first coming—which we now reside in—but at the same time it is not yet in its final form. Jesus' first words in the gospel of Mark are,

> "15 The time is fulfilled, and the kingdom of God is at hand; repent and believe in the gospel." (Mark 1:15)

At the beginning of his ministry, Jesus tells us that God's kingdom has been introduced in himself. The kingdom of God arrived when Jesus arrived. But God's work is in process. It isn't finished.

Theologians have described this concept of God's present kingdom as "already, but not yet…" His kingdom has *already* arrived, but it is *not yet* complete. We still wait for its consummation. So what will that be like?

Everlasting Joy of their Master

Jesus compares our arrival to the New Heavens and New Earth —his finalized kingdom—to a faithful servant entering into his master home. The master looks at the servant and says,

"23 'Well done, good and faithful servant. You have been faithful over a little; I will set you over much. Enter into the joy of your master.'" (Matthew 25:23)

Our blessed hope is that we will hear those words and enter into his perfect and pure, unimpeded presence. We will taste first-hand, the fullness of the eternal joy of our eternal God.

> In your presence there is fullness of joy;
> At your right hand are pleasures forevermore.
> (Psalm 16:11)

By our union with Christ, it's in his presence that we reside and at his right hand we will rule. It's here that affirmation concludes. "…where they will reign with Him forever in the New Heavens and New Earth."

They Will Reign

The Apostle Paul teaches us about the part we play on the other side of death. Part of the blessed hope we have is that we, as God's elect, will not just be playing golf, or reading a wonderful book in heaven. We are taught that we have responsibility. We will rule with Jesus in his consummated kingdom.

11 The saying is trustworthy, for:

> If we have died with him,

we will also live with him;

12 if we endure,

we will also reign with him.

(2 Timothy 2:11-12)

17 ...and if children, then heirs—heirs of God and fellow heirs with Christ, provided we suffer with him in order that we may also be glorified with him. (Romans 8:17)

2 Or do you not know that the saints will judge the world? And if the world is to be judged by you, are you incompetent to try trivial cases? 3 Do you not know that *we are to judge angels*? How much more, then, matters pertaining to this life!

(1 Corinthians 6:2-3)

Do we see that? We are "co-heirs" with Christ. We will "reign" with him. We will "judge" the angels of God. It's at the closing of history that we will come full circle as God's image-bearers. The dominion and rule that Adam was originally given in the garden has been restored in Jesus—the better Adam. And by our faith in him, this dominion has also been given to us in the New Heavens and New Earth.

New Heavens and New Earth

That which was lost, so long ago in that garden, God will restore and renew in the new garden. Through the Apostle John's prophetic hand in the book of Revelation, he lifts the curtain for us so that we could catch a glimpse of the end of the story and what becomes of us.

In the closing pages of *The Bible*, John leads us to the new garden—a garden better than the one in the opening pages. While the garden in Genesis had Adam, the new garden in the New Earth has the better Adam. While the garden in the beginning had two rivers, the new garden has two rivers, but they flow from the throne of God, himself. While the original garden possessed the tree of life, then guarded by the flaming sword, the new garden is placed as the centerpiece to the New Earth with no restriction.

I've heard many say that God is working to get us back to Eden, but that is too low a view of the New Earth. God is not bringing us back to Eden. He's bringing us past Eden into something better. Our blessed hope is to arrive at the city of God—the New Jerusalem—where Christ is its light. And it's there that we will reign with him.

The concluding pages of *The Bible* leave us with this blessed hope.

1 Then I saw a new heaven and a new earth, for the first heaven and the first earth had passed away, and the sea was no more. 2 And I saw the holy city, new Jerusalem, coming down out of heaven from God, prepared as a bride adorned for her husband. 3 And I heard a loud voice from the throne saying, "Behold, the dwelling place of God is with man. He will dwell with them, and they will be his people, and God himself will be with them as their God. 4 He will wipe away every tear from their eyes, and death shall be no more, neither shall there be mourning, nor crying, nor pain anymore, for the former things have passed away." 5 And he who was seated on the throne said, "Behold, I am making all things new." Also he said, "Write this down, for these words are trustworthy and true." 6 And he said to me, "It is done! I am the Alpha and the Omega, the beginning and the end. To the thirsty I will give from the spring of the water of life without payment. (Revelation 21:1-6)

22 And I saw no temple in the city, for its temple is the Lord God the Almighty and the Lamb. 23 And the city has no need of sun or moon to shine on it, for the glory of God gives it light, and its lamp is the Lamb. 24 By its light will the nations walk, and the kings of the earth will bring their glory into it, 25 and its gates will never be shut by day—and there will be no night there. 26 They will bring into it the glory and the honor of the nations. 27 But nothing unclean will ever enter it, nor anyone who does what is detestable or false, but only those who are written in the Lamb's book of life.
(Revelation 21:22-27)

1 Then the angel showed me the river of the water of life, bright as crystal, flowing from the throne of God and of the Lamb 2 through the middle of the street of the city; also, on either side of the river, the tree of life with its twelve kinds of fruit, yielding its fruit each month. The leaves of the tree were for the healing of the nations. 3 No longer will there be anything accursed, but the throne of God and of the Lamb will be in it, and his servants will worship him. 4 They will see his face, and his name will be on their foreheads. 5 And night will be no more. They will need no light of lamp or sun, for the Lord God will be their light, and they will reign forever and ever. (Revelation 22:1-5)

And so we wait for that day with great expectancy.

20 Amen. Come Lord Jesus!

(Revelation 22:20)

Pillar 10 Endnotes

[1] Esoteric Christianity teaches that Christ's return is a resurrection of "Christ within"—that when we become a Christian, Jesus returns in our heart.

[2] Docetism was the early heresy that taught that Jesus' body was not real, but more of an illusion.

[3] Traditional Rastafari doctrine taught that the second coming of Jesus was in a man name Haile Selassie, often referred to as the Black Jesus. This is the belief in a second incarnation.

[4] The word "non-elect" does not appear in scripture. Rather it's a designation used to describe the group in contrast to the "elect".

Afterword

In a day when compromise and concessions prevail, a contemporary rendering of the historic theological pillars of the Church are needed more than ever. Some may ask, "Why do we need a statement of faith?"

I would begin with the popular notion that the world is prone to emotionally believe anything with conviction if it is cradled in the creed "Follow your heart." This dogma is actually a humanistic statement of faith—a mantra in the stream of pop-cultural myths. This humanistic gospel is preached in, classrooms, media platforms, movies, songs, and even many churches. It sounds beautiful, simple and liberating, which explains why it's embraced by billions of people around the world. But our hearts were never designed to be followed. They were designed to be led. Our hearts were never meant to be believed. Rather they were meant to believe—to believe in God.

Whether it's students at the University of Oregon, or the indigenous peoples who forage the muddy jungles of Papua New Guinea, they all follow and believe principles that order their lives. Yet without Christ, their cultures, families and fortunes teeter on shifting sand. (Matthew 7:24-27) But the God of *truth* has spoken concerning Jesus. (Hebrews 1:2) It is his truth that is the objective certainty necessary for grasping God's eternal plan.

Without an understanding of the historic biblical pillars given to us by God, we will continue to cling to wrong notions and remain lost. A stable and maturing life of faith must stand solely on a body of doctrine which has been "delivered to the saints." (Jude 3)

Your elders have not drafted new doctrines for *Redeemer Fellowship*. Rather, we have sought to imitate those who have historically labored to clarify for the saints these spiritual realities, as revealed by God to his Apostles and prophets. (Ephesians 2:20) And we intend to teach those truths to the churches as the "whole counsel of God" (Acts 20:27) or the "standard of teaching." (Romans 6:17)

Jude exhorted the church to "contend for the faith" of which are the key doctrines of Christianity. (Jude 3; 1 Corinthians 9:24). United, your elders agree that these biblical pillars are truths worth dying for. We can imagine dying for a family member or perhaps our country, but to die for *truth* shows the importance we place on these pillars.

This may be challenging for our relativistic culture to comprehend. But when truth is distorted, the glory of God and the message of salvation becomes grotesquely deceptive. The church needs to understand these essential doctrinal pillars, because we love our God and we love making known to the world his amazing and glorious gospel.

With joy, your elders commend Aaron's instructive book and this succinct doctrinal statement to our Great Shepherd, and his bride the Church. It is our prayer that our Lord bless you with a fresh appreciation of our spiritual pillars.

For the Lamb and His Bride,

Dave Baker

Appendix A
Baptism

"18 All authority in heaven and on earth has been given to me. 19 Go therefore and make disciples of all nations, baptizing them in the name of the Father and of the Son and of the Holy Spirit, 20 teaching them to observe all that I have commanded you. And behold, I am with you always, to the end of the age."

(Matthew 28:18-20)

Jesus Commands Baptism

In the Gospel of Matthew Jesus commands that his church make a practice of making disciples of all nations, and *baptize* them in the name of the Father, and of the Son, and of the Holy Spirit. (Matthew 28:19) This is one of the two ordinances that Jesus institutes for his church. Baptism is the first step in following Jesus Christ. So what is baptism?

What is Baptism?

Baptism is the immersion of the body into water. This act represents our death to sin, while our emergence from the water represents our new life with Jesus.

Baptism is a way that we can physically identify with Jesus' death as our death, and his life with our life, by faith in him. *Baptism is the outward sign of an inward reality, which has already taken place by faith in him.*

3 Do you not know that all of us who have been baptized into Christ Jesus were baptized into his death? 4 We were buried therefore with him by baptism into death, in order that, just as Christ was raised from the dead by the glory of the Father, we too might walk in newness of life.

5 For if we have been united with him in a death like his, we shall certainly be united with him in a resurrection like his. 6 We know that our old self was crucified with him in order that the body of sin might be brought to nothing, so that we would no longer be enslaved to sin. 7 For one who has died has been set free from sin. 8 Now if we have died with Christ, we believe that we will also live with him. 9 We know that Christ, being raised from the dead, will never die again; death no longer has dominion over him. 10 For the death he died he died to sin, once for all, but the life he lives he lives to God. 11 So you also must consider yourselves dead to sin and alive to God in Christ Jesus. (Romans 6:3-11; cf. also Colossians 2:12)

Does Baptism Save You?

So, if Jesus commands baptism, does this mean that baptism saves us? No. Baptism doesn't save anyone. It's not a requirement in order to be accepted by God. There is one requirement and that is Jesus himself—his righteousness given to us by faith alone. (Ephesians 2:8-9)

How Does Baptism Bless You?

Finally, why is baptism so important in the context of the local church? There are a few ways that baptism is a means of God's grace, not only for the one being baptized, but for those who witness the baptism as well. In baptism:

- God blesses you and pours out his grace on you with the joy that comes with *obeying your Lord Jesus.* (Psalm 119:47)

- There is a joy in identifying your whole self—body and soul—with Jesus' death and resurrection. There is a fuller joy in not only involving your soul (which can be a private thing), but also involving your whole body in declaring your allegiance to Jesus. (Romans 6:4).

- God blesses your soul when, with your body, you identify with God's work of purifying you from your sins by coming out of the water pure. (Ephesians 5:26-27)

How Does Baptism Bless the Church?

But baptism also blesses others. Through your baptism:

- God blesses *the church* in our witness of a brother or sister walking in obedience to Christ.

- God blesses *the church* in witnessing a brother or sister physically identifying with Jesus' death as their death and Jesus' life as their life.

- God blesses *the church* in witnessing a brother or sister displaying God's work of purifying them from their sin.

Appendix B
PERSONAL TESTIMONY

Why Write a Personal Testimony

This Appendix is for you. There are a couple of reasons why writing out a personal testimony is beneficial and why I've included it as an appendix in this book. The first is that in writing out your testimony, it gives you an opportunity to effectively share with others what the Lord has done for you in a way that avoids confusion or rambling. You are able to better communicate 1) what your life was like before Jesus, 2) how Jesus saved you and the circumstances surrounding your conversion, and 3) what changes God has made in you since you began following Christ.

But more importantly, writing out your personal testimony becomes an act of worship. This exercise is an act of remembrance, reflecting on what the Lord Jesus has done for you in bringing you out of death and into life. Christian heritage is saturated with remembrance. This was the main practice in the Passover holiday, and at the Lord's Table every week in our church. The exercise of writing out your personal testimony is nothing more than an avenue for remembrance as you reflect on the Lord's work, and thus it's a means of worship.

With that said, write. Write in your own words. Write with honesty. Write with passion. Write with wisdom. Write from the mind, into the heart, and onto the page, for the glory of God.

My Personal Testimony

Scripture Index

Genesis

Mark

Luke

John

Acts

Romans

2 Corinthians

Revelation

Made in the USA
Middletown, DE
09 April 2022

63613038R00154